People Who Changed THE WORLD

100
Artists
Who Changed the World

Barbara Krystal

WORLD ALMANAC® LIBRARY

Please visit our web site at: www.worldalmanaclibrary.com
For a free color catalog describing World Almanac® Library's list of high-quality books
and multimedia programs, call 1-800-848-2928 (USA) or 1-800-387-3178 (Canada).
World Almanac® Library's fax: (414) 332-3567.

Library of Congress Cataloging-in-Publication Data

Krystal, Barbara.
    100 artists who changed the world / Barbara Krystal.
      p. cm. — (People who changed the world)
    Includes index.
    Summary: Brief biographies of 100 artists, from ancient Greece to the present
day, who played significant roles in the development of sculpture, painting, and
photography.
    ISBN 0-8368-5469-1 (lib. bdg.)
    1. Artists—Biography—Juvenile literature. [1. Artists.] I. Title: One hundred
artists who changed the world. II. Krystal, Barbara. 100 artists who shaped world
history. III. Title. IV. Series.
N42.K79 2003
709'.2'2—dc21
[B]   2002033153

This North American edition first published in 2003 by
World Almanac® Library
330 West Olive Street, Suite 100
Milwaukee, WI 53212 USA

This U.S. edition © 2003 by World Almanac® Library. Original edition © 1997 by Bluewood
Books. First published by Bluewood Books, A Division of The Siyeh Group, Inc., P.O. Box 689,
San Mateo, CA 94401.

Editor: Richard Michaels
Copy editor: Bob Juran
Designer: Eric Irving
World Almanac® Library editor: Betsy Rasmussen
World Almanac® Library art direction and cover design: Tammy Gruenewald

Cover images from top to bottom: Andy Warhol, Claude Monet, and Georgia O'Keeffe.

Photo credits: Text page illustrations are by Tony Chikes and are © 1997 Bluewood Books
with the following exceptions: Archive Photos: 93, 99, 102, 105; Archive Photos/Archive
France: 91; Archive Photos/Camera Press: 103; Archive Photos/Walter Daran: 97; Archive
Photos/Express Newspaper: 96; Archive Photos/Popperfoto: 95; © Bettmann/CORBIS: 16, 26,
44, 45, 65, 75, 85, 86, 87, 98; © Burckhardt Rudolph/CORBIS SYGMA: 104; © Julia Margaret
Cameron/Hulton Archive: 46; © CORBIS: 88, 107; Courtesy of Sarah G. Epstein Family
Collection: 68; © George Eastman House/Nickolas Muray/Hulton Archive: cover, middle inset,
101; © Darlene Hammond/Getty Images: cover, top inset; © Hulton Archive: 12, 39, 47, 55;
© Hulton-Deutsch Collection/CORBIS: 53; Courtesy of Janet J. LeClair: 72; © Joe Munroe/Getty
Images: cover, bottom inset; © Michael Nicholson/CORBIS: 22; © Ted Streshinsky/CORBIS: 83;
© Roger Viollet/Getty Images: 49, 57, 58, 59, 78; © Oscar White/CORBIS: 82.

Printed in the United States of America

1 2 3 4 5 6 7 8 9 07 06 05 04 03

About the Author: Barbara Krystal resides in the San Francisco Bay Area. She earned a B.A. in English from U.C.
Santa Barbara and is a freelance writer and editor.

TABLE OF CONTENTS

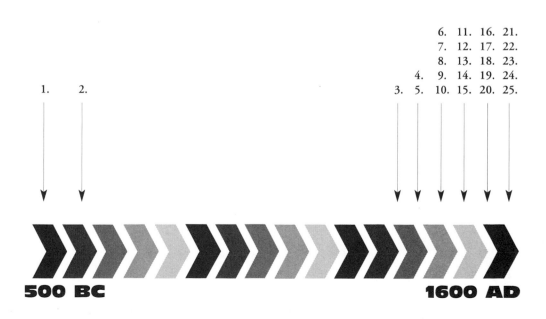

6. 11. 16. 21.
7. 12. 17. 22.
8. 13. 18. 23.
4. 9. 14. 19. 24.
3. 5. 10. 15. 20. 25.

1. 2.

500 BC   1600 AD

TABLE OF CONTENTS

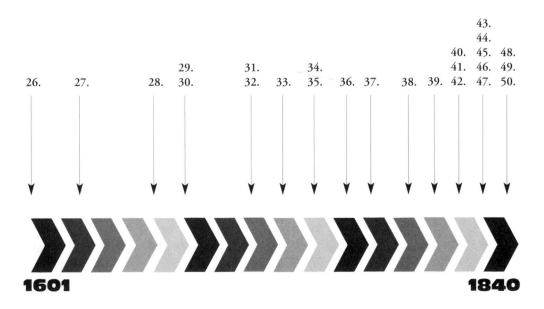

TABLE OF CONTENTS

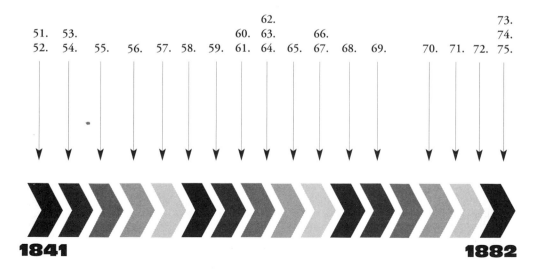

51. 53.
52. 54. 55. 56. 57. 58. 59. 60. 61. 62. 63. 64. 65. 66. 67. 68. 69. 70. 71. 72. 73. 74. 75.

1841   **1882**

TABLE OF CONTENTS

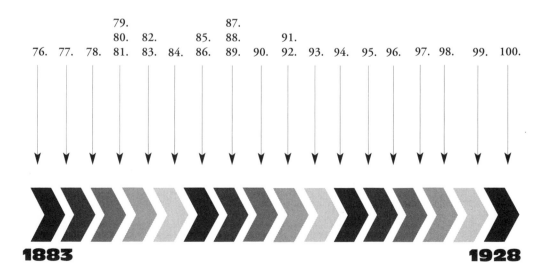

79.
80. 82.   85. 88.   91.
76. 77. 78. 81. 83. 84. 86. 89. 90. 92. 93. 94. 95. 96. 97. 98. 99. 100.

1883   **1928**

ALPHABETICAL
TABLE OF CONTENTS

1. PHIDIAS
(490?–430 B.C.)

The classical period was characterized by an awareness of the role of the individual in determining human destiny. Phidias (FID-ee-us), a Greek sculptor of the classical period, was known for his style of perfection in reproducing ideal beauty of the human form.

Born in Attica, Greece, Phidias was fortunate. Pericles (495–429 B.C.), the head of affairs in the Athenian state, commissioned Phidias's entire artistic career, beginning with the creation of a bronze group of national heroes for Athens. Pericles later made Phidias superintendent of all public works, which allowed him privileges not usually allotted to artists, who were regarded as merchants. Phidias invented new ways of combining figures on foot and on horseback to increase the impression of movement in sculpture.

Phidias exerted a large artistic influence during the era and was the guiding force behind the development of the classical style. The classical style is a term referring to the principles of Greek art that emphasize structure and form. He is credited with the con-struction of the entrance to the Acropolis, known as the Propylaea (pro-pi-LEE-a), where Greek council members met to discuss government affairs. He also supervised and probably designed the construction of the Parthenon, the temple of Athena and the epitome of Greek ideals. Phidias's own contribution to the Parthenon was the gold-and-ivory statue of *Athena*, which was over 40 feet (12 m) in height. The *Athena* is a standing figure; in her left hand she holds a lance, while a shield rests along her left side. Her extended right hand holds the ancient Greek goddess of victory. The shield, pedestal, helmet, and sandals were decorated with scenes from Greek legends. The gold on the statue was detachable to ward off vandals. Detailed descriptions of the statue by ancient authors have preserved its classical beauty.

In studying sculptures in the monuments of Greece, we can see it is almost certain that Phidias completed the famous gold-and-ivory statue of *Zeus at Olympia* after he worked on the Parthenon. The statue depicts the god seated on a dais, holding a scepter in his left hand, while his right hand rests on the relief figure, the "Nike."

In both these works (*Athena* and *Zeus at Olympia*) Phidias employed a technique known as chryselephantine (kris-EL-e-fan-TEEN), in which a core of wood is overlaid with ivory to represent flesh, and gold inlaid with enamel is used for the drapery.

The events of Phidias's last years are disputed. Some accounts say that he was imprisoned until his death after being accused by the enemies of Pericles of embezzling gold that had been set aside for the completion of the statue of Athena. Another account says that he was acquitted of the charges of embezzlement but was condemned for blasphemy after putting his own portrait on the shield of the goddess Athena.

Phidias in his study

2. PRAXITELES
(390?–330 B.C.)

At a time when sculptors were simply entrepreneurs operating shops in the marketplace like any other vendor, Praxiteles (prak-SIT-e-lees) emerged as an extraordinary artist. He elevated art above the simple notion that a sculptor was just another businessperson selling wares.

Praxiteles, the son of the sculptor Kephisodotus, was considered the leader of the Attic school of art. Concentrating on marble statues, he set the precedent for style and content that others would soon follow. Praxiteles was one of the first to become aware of the translucent nature of marble, which enabled him to create more lifelike images.

Renowned for his humanization of Greek art, Praxiteles used the lesser-known deities, such as Aphrodite, the goddess of love, and Hermes, the messenger to the gods, for his work. His disillusionment with community values and concern for life came about as a result of the constant fighting and wars among the Greek city-states. These conflicts turned his artistic taste toward the view that mankind's well-being and happiness in this lifetime are primary, and the good of all humanity is the highest ethical goal; thus, his portrayals of divinities do not possess the superhuman qualities of earlier Greek works.

It is possible that one of his original works still exists. *Hermes Holding the Infant Dionysos* was found during the excavation of the Temple of Hera in Olympia, Greece, in 1877, where the author Pausanias had described seeing it more than 1,700 years before. Although the find may be only a good Roman copy, it lends insight to Praxiteles and the manner in which he expressed himself. His signature pieces all contained a languid curve to the figure, resembling the letter "S," and so termed the

Praxiteles

Praxitelean curve. His most celebrated work, the marble statue of Aphrodite, which survives as a Roman copy in the Vatican Museum in Italy, was the first nude statue of the goddess and one of the earliest Greek statues of a female nude. This demonstrates the change in the status of women and Praxiteles's role as an artist to convey that change openly in tangible form. He is especially celebrated for his satyr; the best known is the *Resting Satyr*, of which a Roman copy exists in the Capitol Museum in Rome, Italy. A satyr is a god of the woods with the head and body of a man and the legs, ears, and horns of a goat. It was immortalized in 1860 in the book *The Marble Faun*, by author Nathaniel Hawthorne.

Cimabue

The art of painting had fallen into decay in Italy during the thirteenth century. Cimabue (che-ma-BOO-a), a Florence-born painter, resurrected the art by painting from living models, which was considered a new thing at the time. Documents show that his real name was Bencivieni di Pepo, or, in modern Italian, Benvenuto di Giuseppe. At the time, it was common to adopt nicknames and use them throughout one's lifetime. "Cima" has two meanings; the noun means summit or head, and the verb means to shear or cut. The suffix "bue" means ox. Thus, his name would signify an "ox head," a bold and stubborn man. The name suited him, as pointed out by Dante (1265-1321), author of the book *The Divine Comedy*. Dante wrote: "Cimabue, a painter of our time, is a man so arrogant and proud withal, that if any discovered a fault in his work, or if he perceived one in himself, as will often happen to the artist who fails from the defects in material that he uses, or from insufficiency of the instrument with which he works, he would instantly abandon that work, however costly it might be."

Cimabue was an influential painter who broke away from the formalism of Byzantine art, characterized by rigid and fictitious representations of nature. He introduced a lifelike treatment of traditional religious subjects by replacing conventional design with a more vital manner of painting based on his observations of real things. His signature mark is a partly angular, partly curved structure that conveys movement and energy and was a precursor of dimension in art. It is speculated that Cimabue earned the title of "wall painter" for his expansion of the style of monumental scale painting of his older contemporary, Coppo di Marcovaldo. His most noted work is the *Madonna Enthroned* (1285?), which is over 12 feet (7 m) high; it was certainly a feat for a time that focused on small canvas paintings. Cimabue is generally placed by art historians at the beginning of modern art and as the probable teacher of Giotto (1266–1337), a Florentine painter who achieved a representation of space without using a system of perspective common in the Byzantine formula of art. Cimabue is known to have visited Rome in 1272, and he was perhaps influenced by the classical current in art that was prevalent there at the time. Cimabue is recorded in historical documents for the commission of the painting *Crucifix* (1260?) for the hospital church of St. Chiara, Pisa, Italy, and as a master workman on the mosaic of *St. John* (1301?) at the Pisa Cathedral. Many frescoes have been attributed to him, although modern scholars accept only a few as authentic. The majority of his works are located in the Church of St. Francesco at Assisi, Italy.

4. DONATELLO
(1386?–1466)

Renowned for creating sculptures that exemplified the qualities of the Renaissance period, such as experimentation, invention, and creativity, Donato di Niccolo di Betto Bardi, known as Donatello, was recognized in his early twenties as a prolific artist. He is regarded as the founder of modern sculpture due to his innovation in optical illusion. Donatello's technique made the eye actually see what was there, instead of the viewer imagining what seemed to be there. His technique was to cut into the clay, using protrusions to reflect light or shadow to produce the effect of proximity or distance to the eye.

Born in Florence, Italy, the son of a wool comber, Donatello began an art career at age seventeen as an apprentice to the sculptor Lorenzo Ghiberti

Donatello

(1378–1455). He assisted in decorating the doors in the baptistery of San Giovanni, Florence. The work brought him into association with the architect Filippo Brunelleschi (1377–1466), who gave Donatello the opportunity to visit Rome between 1408 and 1412 to study the ancient sculptures.

Donatello's career marks the transition from medieval sculpture, which was overtly religious in context and created in the service of the church, to sculpture that glorified man as a youth, warrior, and saint. Based on the study of human anatomy and movement, Donatello was able to show emotion in his sculptures, emphasizing the poses of his figures and the space around them.

A story is told of Donatello destroying a bronze head made for a Florence merchant who objected to the price. The merchant argued that Donatello had spent only a month on the project, therefore he was entitled to a typical month's wage. Donatello was outraged that his work was measured in terms of hours spent and destroyed the sculpture.

He created free-standing figures, fountains, and animals. He used clay, bronze, or marble. He also varied scale.

Donatello's career is normally divided into three periods. The first period comprises the time between seventeen and thirty-nine years of age and is characterized by the influence of Gothic sculpture, referring to a style invoking the effect of mystery. His famous work of this time was *St. John the Evangelist* (1415), made for the facade of the Florence Cathedral. The second period dates from the years 1425–1435, in which Donatello made trips to Rome. The bronze *David* (1435) is considered the first life-size, free-standing nude statue of the Renaissance. In his third period, Donatello emphasized realism and the portrayal of dramatic action. His sculpture *Judith and Holofernes* (1461) shows the integration of two figures in a single sculpture.

Donatello emphasized art as a reproduction of reality; for example, he created the drapery for the figure of Judith by dipping a real cloth into wax. Believing that an artist must be able to "feel deeply and translate those feelings into concrete form," Donatello had the ability to create a sense of life in his work.

5. JAN VAN EYCK
(1390?–1441)

Jan van Eyck (van-IKE), a Flemish painter, is the founder of the style known as ars nova (new art). Uncertainty regarding van Eyck's early training exists. There has been debate and speculation among scholars regarding the authenticity of some of his paintings, creating a rumor that van Eyck's brother Hubert had a hand in creating some of the more problematic and detailed of the paintings. Van Eyck's greatest masterpiece, the *Ghent Altarpiece* (1432) for the Cathedral of Saint Bavon, Ghent, was commissioned by the mayor of Brugge, Belgium, Jodocus Vyt. The work consists of two superimposed rows of painting, bearing an inscription that indicates that the piece was begun by Hubert and completed by Jan. Hubert died in 1426, and it is presumed that Jan van Eyck took many of Hubert's unfinished works and completed them.

Jan van Eyck was born in Maaseick, in the province of Limburg, Belgium. His groundbreaking work combined fantasy and illusion

Jan van Eyck

with reality in common, everyday scenes. He proclaimed that the novelty of Flemish art lay in the belief that humans, nature, and social daily life were fascinating subjects when composed in a spiritual unity.

Van Eyck was the first to use the optical phenomenon known as atmospheric perspective. Atmospheric perspective is a perception of space and the limit of visibility, serving to add continuity to a painting. The Italian humanist Bartolomeo Fazio called van Eyck the "prince of painters of our age." In 1422, he entered the service of John of Bavaria, count of Holland, as official court painter. After John's death in 1425, van Eyck became *valet de chambre* to Philip the Good, Duke of Burgundy. By the time he was thirty-five, he had already earned the title of master, which was unusual for someone that young. He was both painter and trusted diplomat to Philip. Van Eyck participated in many long and secret journeys for Philip, including a trip in 1428 to Portugal to negotiate a marriage between Philip and Princess Isabella, daughter of King John I.

Van Eyck represented the new artist—the artist as an intellectual and master of other arts. In 1430, he settled for good in Brugge, where he began to sign and date his work for the first time. Van Eyck was also a chemist of sorts, and he is credited with the invention of a type of oil paint that allowed him to develop precise technical skills. These skills earned him the reputation as "king of painters" by fellow citizens well into the sixteenth century.

Although controversy exists as to the authenticity of much of his work, van Eyck's name is noted in history as the great pioneer of Flemish realism. Nine paintings by van Eyck are still in existence, all carefully signed and dated between 1432 and 1439. Five are portraits. The other four depict religious subjects, including the *Madonna with Canon van der Paele* (1436).

6. GIOVANNI BELLINI
(1430?–1516)

Giovanni Bellini, the Italian painter from the city of Venice, belonged to an artistic family. He was born out of wedlock to the painter Jacopo Bellini (1400?–1470), who emphasized the Renaissance style of perspective, landscape, and classical beauty. Bellini was the younger brother of the painter Gentile Bellini (1429–1507), renowned for his portraits and his skillful arrangement of crowds standing before detailed architectural structures. Another major influence on Bellini was his brother-in-law Andrea Mantegna (1431–1506), a painter whose work is noted for its illusion of realistic depth.

Bellini began his artistic career by assisting his father in the family workshop. By twenty-nine years of age, he had ventured out on independent projects and opened a workshop of his own. Bellini was famous for religious paintings. His perception of color and light, rather than emphasis on line, defined his sensitivity to minute details. Bellini's immense talent, connections, and family reputation gained him immediate success. His first works as an independent artist were *Agony in the Garden* (1460) and *Man of Sorrows* (1460?). At this point, Bellini's work emphasized the use of light, facial expressions to convey emotions, and body language to dramatize the scene. In 1480, he was given an annual salary when he was appointed chief painter to the Venetian Republic, a position he maintained until his death. Bellini's duties included executing official portraits of court personages and portraying historical events. As official painter of the court, he was not paid an extra commission for his work. Simultaneously, Bellini maintained his own studio and a large workshop of pupils, which included the famous painters Titian (1487–1576) and Giorgione (1476–1510). Bellini's signature OP. IOH.BELL. became the trademark of the shop as well as of the paintings he created on his own. This later led to

Giovanni Bellini

confusion concerning the origin of different works.

Bellini did not travel, yet he exerted an international influence. Students journeyed across the European continent to apprentice with him and then returned to their homes taking Bellini's style with them. It was during his time as chief painter to the Venetian Republic that he adopted a technique of oil painting that lessened the distinction between solids and space. A gradual transition of light and shadow replaced lines. The works that depict these changes are *St. Francis* (1480) and *Madonna of the Trees* (1487). Gradually, Bellini's style was built entirely in forms of solid objects, where three-dimensional space was emphasized. The style is represented in the altarpiece *The Virgin and Child and Four Saints* (1483), where the illusions of depth are prominent. Bellini's ideal was to produce images composed entirely in terms of color, rather than line.

7. HUGO VAN DER GOES
(1440?–1482)

Hugo van der Goes

Regarded as one of the greatest fifteenth-century Flemish painters, Hugo van der Goes introduced emotional intensity and deep sentimentality into his religious subject matter. Van der Goes was born in Ghent, Belgium. He painted there and entered the artists' guild at age twenty-seven. At age thirty-four, he became dean of the guild. The earliest works of his career are *The Fall of Man* (1467?) and the *Lamentation* (1468?), which are regarded as his official induction into the art world. In 1468, on behalf of the guild, he went to Brugge, Belgium to aid in decorating the city for the marriage of Margaret of York and Charles the Bold. From this experience, he earned an esteemed reputation that enabled him to attract patrons from among the prominent citizens of Brugge, as well as continual employment from Margaret and Charles. At the same time, van der Goes created paintings for the church of St. Pharahildis for the funeral ser-vices of Philip the Good, Duke of Burgundy, and his wife, Princess Isabella of Portugal, in 1473.

Despite his worldly success, he retired to the Red Cloister monastery near Brussels as a lay brother at thirty-five years of age, but he maintained considerable privileges normally not allotted to members of the monastery. Having given all his worldly possessions to the monastery, he was allowed to continue painting. He also drank wine at the table and entertained visitors and patrons of royal esteem. He was permitted to travel outside the walls of the monastery for brief periods of time. He was a deeply religious man, but his fame and extravagant life were incompatible with his ideal of achieving humility. This incompatibility later caused him to experience a severe mental collapse, followed by an attempt at suicide in 1481.

Unable to concentrate and believing that he was going to leave his paintings in an imperfect state on Earth, he continued to decline mentally until his death.

Van der Goes's paintings are not numerous, but all of his paintings are marked by disordered feeling and rich colors. The most firmly dated of his works is the *Portinari Altarpiece* (1476). At over 8 feet (2 m) tall and 19 feet (6 m) wide, this piece was considered enormous by Flemish standards. It was received with disdain because of its size. The entire composition of the portrait centers around the figure of Christ, where the light is concentrated. It also displays an emotional intensity not seen in previous Flemish paintings. The action of the shepherds entering the scene and the gaze of Christ's mother, Mary, creates a feeling of tension in the piece. The painting was commissioned by the Medici, the ruling family of Italy, and brought van der Goes fame in Florence, placing him prominently in the history of Italian painting.

8. BOTTICELLI
(1445?–1510)

Alessandro Filipepi, known as Sandro Botticelli (bot-e-CHEL-ee), was born in Florence, Italy. As one of the leading painters of the Italian renaissance, his paintings reflected the popular thought that the soul gains ultimate knowledge and truth by withdrawing into itself. He was the youngest of five sons of Mariano Filipepi, a tanner. It is presumed that he received his nickname *Botticelli*, meaning "little barrel," from the name of the goldsmith to whom he was first apprenticed. Botticelli later served an apprenticeship with the painter and monk Fra Filippo Lippi (1406–1469). Lippi is famous for his altarpieces and is credited with helping Botticelli develop his personal style, which emphasizes line, detail, and a sense of melancholy.

By the time Botticelli was fifteen years old, he had his own workshop. He spent almost all of his life working for the great families of Florence, especially the Medici, the ruling family of Italy. For the Medici, he painted portraits. *The Adoration of the Magi* (1477) is representative of the influence of the circle of the Medici family. Although the work was not commissioned by the Medici, a vast number of figures contain likenesses of personages of the royal court. The painting depicts figures pantomiming in animated poses, detracting from the focus of the central subject. The piece expresses Botticelli's desire to create a world

Sandro Botticelli

where value is placed on intellect and morality.

As part of the artistic circle at the court of Lorenzo de Medici (1449–1492), Botticelli was influenced by philosophers and other inhabitants of the court. Through this influence, he reconciled classical pagan and Christian views. The most famous depiction of this experience is *The Birth of Venus* (1482?), which symbolizes both positions on love. The painting depicts the goddess Venus emerging from a seashell. Proportions of anatomy are ignored, as the body is elongated and the length of the arms and legs are exaggerated. This style invokes a feeling of movement that is free from control and appears to be under the natural influence of gravity. The weight of the body is distributed unequally, so the figure conforms to a single continuous curve.

In 1481, Botticelli was chosen to travel to Rome to paint the three frescoes—*The Youth of Moses, The Punishment of the Sons of Corah*, and *The Temptation of Christ*—as well as papal portraits. It was during this time that Botticelli underwent a religious awakening, manifesting itself in a devotion to the church and the painting of religious subjects. *Mystic Nativity* (1501) and *Stories of St. Zenobius* (1505?) both expressed his enthusiasm for the church.

9. LEONARDO DA VINCI
(1452–1519)

Leonardo da Vinci

Celebrated as a painter, sculptor, architect, engineer, and scientist, Leonardo da Vinci (da-VIN-chee) was truly the quintessential Renaissance man. His talents characterized the ideals of ingenuity and creativity. For Leonardo, there was no authority greater than the eye, which he characterized as the "window of the soul."

He was born out of wedlock in Vinci, a Tuscan village, to a wealthy Florentine notary, Piero da Vinci, and a peasant woman identified only as Caterina. At age fourteen, Leonardo was apprenticed as a *garzone*, or "studio boy," to Andrea del Verrocchio. Verrocchio taught Leonardo the fundamentals of painting and introduced him to the task of completing works for altarpieces and panel pictures. He also introduced Leonardo to the creation of marble and bronze structures. By the time Leonardo was twenty, he was indoctrinated into the painters' guild and became an independent master six years later.

His first large painting, *The Adoration of the Magi* (1481), was left unfinished but stands apart in its organized rhythm, excellent drawing, and sentiment.

Having written the Duke of Milan a letter claiming he could build portable bridges, construct catapults, make cannons, and build armored vehicles, he entered the world of royalty around 1482, where he remained for seventeen years. It was at this time that he developed his style and labored on his masterpiece, *The Last Supper* (1495). Incorporating drama into the depiction of Christ's disciples receiving testament that Christ was to die, the painting was elaborately calculated to capture the reaction of each disciple individually and as a group in a chain reaction of shock. He grouped the figures in units of three, framing the figure of Christ, who is presented as the only calm subject.

In 1502, Leonardo returned to Florence and was employed as chief architect and engineer by Cesare Borgia, Duke of Romagna. During his employment with the duke, Leonardo painted his most celebrated portrait, the world-famous *Mona Lisa* (1506), also known as *La Gioconda*. The painting is famed for da Vinci's mastery of technical innovations, as well as for the mysterious smiling woman who is the subject. Leonardo used the background, an imaginary landscape of mountains and valley, as a psychological reference to the woman in the forefront. His unique style in the painting gives the impression that the solidity of an object is diminished as it recedes into the distance. The work incorporates the method known as *sfumato*, the Italian word for "smoke," which is the subtle transition between color areas to create an atmospheric haze. The painting also incorporates chiaroscuro (kee-ar-e-SKYOOR-o), a technique of defining forms through contrasts of light and shadow.

In 1507, Leonardo became court painter to King Louis XII of France, who was residing in Milan, Italy at the time. Nine years later, Leonardo went to France to work in the royal court of King Francis I, where he spent the last three years of his life.

ALBRECHT DÜRER
(1471–1528)

Artists of fifteenth-century Germany either followed their fathers into a profession or were apprenticed to friends of the family in similar fields. Third-born in a line of eighteen children in Nuremberg, Germany, Albrecht Dürer had hereditary talent and a father who introduced him to an artistic career by teaching him the craft of a goldsmith. At age thirteen, he drew a remarkable self-portrait and said, "I drew myself while facing the mirror in the year 1484, when I was still a child."

Dürer was an engraver, draftsman, painter, and theorist, often referred to as the northern Leonardo da Vinci (see no. 9). He received his early training in art from the painter and woodcut designer Michael Wolgemut. Upon leaving Wolgemut's studio, Dürer wandered through Germany and Switzerland as a journeyman, working as a woodcut designer in book-publishing centers. Returning to Nuremberg at the age of twenty-three, he established his own workshop as a painter and engraver on copper and wood.

Dürer's fame derives from his depiction of biblical events in human fashion, breaking the limitations of an idyllic church conception. The style is apparent in the sixteen engravings of *Apocalypse of St. John* (1498), of which one plate depicts the battle of the archangel Michael with a dragon, where the figures are formless. As a painter, Dürer's aim was to elevate art above the status of a manufacturing business, to which it had degenerated. *The Adoration of the Magi* (1504) is the most devout of his works and includes a landscape painted directly from nature.

Aware that he was handsome, Dürer had a fondness for self-portraits, which also manifested in his attempt to create a high position for artists in society. In his time, self-portraits existed only as an exercise using oneself as a convenient model. In one self-portrait of 1500, Dürer compared himself to Christ. For Dürer,

a deeply religious man, the artist was a vessel of God because he was the recipient of the gift of creating art.

He also studied theory on the laws of nature with the belief that "art lies hidden in nature; he who can wrest it from her possesses art." *The Fall of Man* (1504) is a synthesis of the natural world, accurate in the portrayal of animals and plants; however, the figures of Adam and Eve show perfect proportions of the human body. In painting, Dürer was part intellect and part mystic, as he examined the system of growth of a plant, the function of the body, and the use of clothing as expression.

At forty-two years of age, his career climaxed with the engraving *Melencolia I* (1514?), which questions the intellectual virtues of science and art. *Melencolia I* shows the figure of Genius surrounded by a disarray of scientific instruments, signifying that Genius is a condition of power and helplessness.

Albrecht Dürer

Michelangelo

During his long life-time, Italian sculptor, painter, and architect Michelangelo Buonarroti was a friend of princes, most notably Lorenzo de Medici (1449–1492), ruler of Florence. He also knew cardinals, popes, painters, and poets. Michelangelo was the son of the governor of Caprese, Lodovico Buonarroti, who had connections with the ruling Medici family. At age thirteen, Michelangelo began an apprenticeship with the painter Domenico Ghirlandaio (1449–1494), who painted religious themes with bourgeois settings and details. In the first of the two years he spent with Ghirlandaio, Michelangelo was involved in a fist fight with a fellow student and received a blow to his nose that left it permanently flattened and crooked.

Thought of as ugly, he was painfully aware of his disfigurement and determined to glorify the male human figure in sculpture. By the time he was sixteen, he had produced the sculptures *Battle of the Centaurs* (1492) and *Madonna of the Stairs* (1492), demonstrating his development of a personal style.

Michelangelo ventured to Rome after the death of Lorenzo de Medici and completed the *Pieta* (1500), one of the few works he ever signed, in St. Peter's Basilica. The work depicts a young Mary, the mother of Christ, with restrained emotion, rather than extreme grief, while she holds the dead Christ in her arms. Michelangelo further demonstrated his talent for large sculpture with the marble *David* (1504), 18 feet (5 m) in height, depicted as a nude youth, muscular and alert. The intensity of the facial expression on David, characteristic of Michelangelo's work, is termed terribilita, which means containing qualities that inspire fear and awe. The same could be attributed to Michelangelo's own personality. In 1505, after the completion of David, Michelangelo was called to Rome by Pope Julius II to paint the frescoes of the Sistine Chapel ceiling. From 1508 to 1512, lying on his back on scaffolding, Michelangelo detailed the story of Creation on a ceiling over 5,800 square feet (539 sq m) in size. The images demonstrate a close scrutiny of human anatomy and movement in the nine scenes from the book of Genesis in the Bible, including *God Separating Light from Darkness*, *Creation of Adam and Eve*, *Temptation and Fall of Adam and Eve*, and *Flood*. The two greatest figures in the scenes are David and Adam, expressing Michelangelo's idea of "divine beauty on Earth."

Michelangelo continued to contribute to the Sistine Chapel, executing the largest fresco of the Renaissance with the portrait of the *Last Judgment* (1541) on the altar wall. Michelangelo portrayed all the figures nude, but a decade later another artist, dubbed the "breeches maker," was commissioned to add draperies to the figures.

As chief architect to St. Peter's Basilica in Rome, Michelangelo was responsible for the final form of the dome. The dome became a symbol of authority and a model for domes throughout the Western world, including the U.S. Capitol in Washington, D.C.

12. MATTHIAS GRÜNEWALD
(1475?–1528)

The technique of the German painter Matthias Grünewald is still thought to be unsurpassed. The genius of Grünewald is said to have been his ability to transform tragedy into something of respect and dignity. The Renaissance had a liberating influence, allowing him to work without theoretical foundations and rational standards, which earned him the appellation of "a wild unpruned tree." This refers to Grünewald's tendency to work according to simple rules, rather than theorized proofs.

Born in Wurzburg, Germany, as Mathis Gothardt Niethardt, he adopted the name Grünewald as a derivation to suggest godliness and dropped his surname of Niethardt, feeling that it had implications of a strict and miserly person. Grünewald's earliest dated work is *The Mocking of Christ* (1504). The painting illustrates Christ blindfolded and beaten by a group of hideous-looking men. A colorful and expressive piece, it demonstrates Grünewald's use of distorted figures to portray violence.

His masterpiece, the *Isenheim Altarpiece* (1515), for the hospital church of the Order of St. Anthony at Isenheim, was an expression of Christian mysticism. It consisted of nine panels mounted on two sets of folding wings with three views; each panel is over 8 feet (2 m) high. The drama of the scene symbolized the divine and human nature of Christ through the use of contrast between a vibrant and light foreground to a dark sky and bleak, low mountain landscape in the background. When the wings of the painting are opened, the scenes of the *Annunciation*, the *Angel Concert for Madonna*, and the *Resurrection* are revealed, demonstrating Grünewald's talent in using light to invoke emotion and the use of writhing forms to create movement. The hospital for which he painted the portrait received patients with mental disorders, and Grünewald's compassion for these individuals with hallucinating minds transformed their hysteria into glory.

Educated as an architect and engineer, a specialist in the design of fountains and mills, he used these skills to support himself after he was discharged from his position as a court painter due to his conversion to Protestantism. Of all the masters of this period, he was deliberately avoided by his contemporaries, since his career as a painter was cut short when he became an antagonist to his patron Albrecht of Brandenburg, who was upset by the fervent change in religious practices occurring in Germany.

He was apparently torn between his sympathy with the peasants and his natural religiosity, shown by the fact that after his death, two rosaries were found in his luggage along with a library of Lutheran literature.

Matthias Grünewald

13. RAPHAEL
(1483–1520)

Raphael

Regarded as the central painter of religious figures of the High Renaissance, Raffaello Santi or Sanzio, commonly known as Raphael (RAF-eye-el), was born in Urbino, Italy into a family of painters. He received his early training in art from his father, Giovanni Santi, a painter and poet who died when Raphael was twelve. At age sixteen, Raphael became a student of the painter Perugino (1445–1523), who was renowned for his simplicity and harmonious symmetrical designs and whom Raphael imitated in style so closely that it is difficult to determine which paintings were completed by which individual.

Using this uncluttered style and emphasizing space, Raphael painted *The Vision of a Knight* (1504). The picture shows a knight asleep under a tree. The scene is divided into two parts, presenting a symbolism of choice. One side represents intellect and morality, illustrated by the figure of a girl holding a book and a staff. The other half presents an alluring woman offering the symbol of the primrose, which signifies irresponsibility and pleasure.

After learning what he could from his teacher, Raphael left for Florence to study the masters Leonardo da Vinci (see no. 9) and Michelangelo (see no. 11). There he developed his style of expressing light and shade, anatomy, and dramatic action.

Raphael's first royal patronage came at a time when the center of the art world was shifting in Italy from Florence to Rome. This shift occurred because the Church wanted to demonstrate its wealth and power in decorating the city of Rome. When Raphael was twenty-six years old, Pope Julius II commissioned him to execute four frescoes in the Vatican Palace. These frescoes represented the personifications of Theology, Philosophy, Art, and Justice. Raphael included his own portrait among the famous personages pictured there, such as the philosophers Plato (427–347 B.C.) and Socrates (470–399 B.C.) and the artist Michelangelo, who at the time was painting his famous *Story of Creation* on the ceiling of the Sistine Chapel. At the death of Pope Julius and the accession of Pope Leo X in 1513, the responsibilities increased for Raphael. He was made chief architect of St. Peter's Basilica in 1514, and a year later, he was appointed director of all excavations of antiquities in Rome.

Raphael's death at the age of thirty-seven was attributed to excessive indulgences. He had several romantic affairs and an active social life not depicted in his works. It was noted that at times he would not give his full attention to a project due to the distraction of the need to be with his mistress. He never married, stating that "marriage was something that could wait until the proper combination of material advantage and personal attraction came along."

14. CORREGGIO
(1489?–1534)

Antonio Allegri, known as Correggio for the town in Italy where he was born and died, created innovations in depicting space and movement in painting. He was considered the forerunner of the baroque style of art that emphasized extravagant and flamboyant scenes. Correggio's paintings are characterized by sensuous nude figures, representing religious and mythological subjects. He enjoyed great popularity in his town, but he had no disciples and exerted little influence in art for a period of one hundred years. He did find valuable patrons in Federigo Gonzaga and Isabella d'Este, both royal members of the court in Mantua, Italy. Another important patron was Giovanna di Piacenza, the headmistress of the convent of San Paolo in Parma, Italy. Correggio was commissioned to paint a set of frescoes for her living quarters. He produced an allegory on the pagan theme of Diana, goddess of the hunt. This work is notable for his use of light and shadow to enhance the illusionary technique.

In the dome of the Cathedral in Parma is Correggio's most famous painting, *Assumption of the Virgin* (1530). With its swirling clouds and intertwined figures flying toward heaven, the painting demonstrates the vastness and action that was to become an art movement. He was thirty-two years old when he completed this work, and he was from then on considered a master. He developed an early interest in art by watching his uncle Lorenzo, who was a painter, grind and mix colors. Carreggio's career differed from those of other painters of the Renaissance period—not by the fact that he had little if any formal training, but by the fact that his art blossomed in one place. Correggio did not travel but worked and lived in his own small province of Parma. There is no proof that Correggio ever visited Rome, although his art seems to show an influence of the ideas of Leonardo da Vinci, Michelangelo, and Raphael (see nos. 9, 11, and 13).

Correggio's paintings serve as a guide to his personality, for there are no written records on his life. One story says he is the descendant of an aristocratic family, while another states that he was a man of simple background. Numerous records exist either in his name or on his behalf, but these contracts and payments do not include dates. His name also appears as a member of a board appointed to study how to remedy structural failures in a church in Parma.

As an artist, Correggio never made the distinction between sacred and pagan subjects. Each is painted in a sensuous pose, showing mystical qualities. An official at the Cathedral in Parma was offended by the painting *Assumption of the Virgin* because of legs floating in the sky. He said that the work was "a frog's leg stew." The famous painter Titian, however, defended the work, saying, "If you turned the dome upside down and filled it with gold pieces they would not equal the worth of Correggio's masterpiece." About forty of Correggio's paintings still exist. The most popular are *Jupiter and Io* (1530?) and *Jupiter and Antiope* (1532?).

Correggio

Benvenuto CELLINI, sculpteur et orfèvre
né en 1500, mort en 1571 à Florence
Œuvres : Nymphe de Fontainebleau, Persée,
Jupiter Tonnant, etc.

Benvenuto Cellini

Equally skilled as a goldsmith, sculptor, and metal worker of the High Renaissance, Benvenuto Cellini (chel-LEE-nee), born in Florence, Italy, did not follow in his father's profession as an architect. He acquired the skill to make intricate designs on shields and swords as an apprentice to the goldsmith Antonio di Sandro at the age of fifteen. Although he is respected as a sculptor, the elaborate detail of his work was more appropriate for metal work at the time. Renowned for possessing a fiery temper and instigating street brawls, at age sixteen he was exiled to Siena but fled to Rome.

Cellini wrote his autobiography (published in 1728), *The Life of Benvenuto Cellini*, which spanned the period roughly between 1538 and 1562. In this book, he provides accounts of his turbulent life and his version of the daily political and social atmosphere in the sixteenth century. It is full of extravagant recordings of his escapades, relaying a vivid picture of his complex personality and stating his mastery at using a sword as well as designing one. He traveled to France in 1540, where he was employed by King Francis I. There he completed an elaborate gold salt cellar sculpture in 1543, depicting the figures of the god Neptune and the goddess Cybele and modeled after the style of Michelangelo (see no. 11). Cellini was compelled to leave France due to his constant quarrels with the king's mistress. Upon his return to Florence, he won the support of Duke Cosimo de Medici and concentrated on making full-scale sculptures in the classical style.

His most important work during this period was *Perseus* (1554), who holds the head of Medusa in his hand. The niches on the base of the statue depict small figures of gods and demonstrate the detail of his metal work. Also of this period was the *Bust of Bindo Aldoviti* (1550?), completed in bronze and representative of a classic style in sculpture. Remorseful of his fiery character, he entered a monastery at age fifty-eight to take a respite from his exploits. But two years of peaceful solitude were sufficient for him, and he then resumed his familiar lifestyle. At age sixty-four, he married his housekeeper, Pierra di Parigi, and had two children, settling for a life of quiet comfort until his death.

16. TINTORETTO
(1518–1594)

Jacopo Robusti was given the name *Tintoretto*, meaning "little dyer," in allusion to his father's profession as a dyer of silk. Essentially a self-taught painter, Tintoretto created monumental religious murals, characterized by exaggerated body movements and strong contrasts of light and shade. Tintoretto was a Venetian mannerist painter who lived and worked exclusively in Venice, Italy, for the rulers and churches of that city.

He began his career under the tutelage of Titian (1487?–1576). He stayed for ten days, but the constant arguments between the two caused Tintoretto's expulsion from the studio. Tintoretto found himself ostracized from the art community after he left Titian's studio, and he was therefore severed from the possibility of obtaining public and private commissions.

Without formal training, Tintoretto searched for a style and discovered diverse sources of inspiration. Through the study of Michelangelo (see no. 11) and other Florentine mannerist painters, he developed his own impression and created a sense of spontaneous action. His developed a style focused on spatial illusions and extravagant choreographic groupings to heighten the drama of an event. His painting *St. Mark Rescuing a Slave* (1848) was a dramatic departure from tradition.

Described as a showman in paint, Tintoretto's bold colors and bizarre angles made the majority of painters in Venice shun him, forcing him to adopt aggressive methods of self-promotion. He brought his work to public attention by seeking well-situated homes or business stalls and offering to paint their front entrances for free. He had an impulsive character and gave his paintings away to anyone who genuinely admired them. In 1549, he accepted, as partial payment for work he had done for a monastery, admission to its membership as a way to make connections with some who might appreciate him.

Intense religiosity moved Tintoretto toward an expressive narrative style in art. He used distortions of normal relationships in space and between people to strengthen the importance of the subjects and to convey meaning and mood; the most famous example is *Crucifixion* (1569). This painting shows a setting confined to a narrow strip, behind which a group of bystanders, silhouetted against a darkening sky, rise to view the body of Christ.

On the occasion of the visit of King Henry III of France to Venice, when Tintoretto was fifty-six years old, Tintoretto disguised himself as one of the king's bodyguards to get close enough to make sketches for a portrait. Upon the portrait's completion, Tintoretto refused the king's offer to make him a knight.

Tintoretto continued to paint until his death. The last completed painting was *Entombment* (1594).

Tintoretto

17. GIUSEPPE ARCIMBOLDO
(1527?–1593)

Giuseppe Arcimboldo

Giuseppe Arcimboldo (ar-chim-BOL-do) painted satirical portraits of court personages and famous personalities of the past. He was thought to be the foreshadower of twentieth century surrealist art, which emphasized the unconscious, for his paintings of animals, flowers, fruit, and other objects composed to form human likenesses. Commencing an artistic career as a designer of stained glass and tapestry in Milan, Italy, the place of his birth, he moved to Prague, Czechoslovakia, at age thirty-five, where he became the official painter of the Hapsburg court. He began his service under Ferdinand I and remained a court painter to that monarch's successors,

Maximillian II and Rudolph II, for a total of twenty-six years. Rudolph II greatly admired Arcimboldo's work and named him a Count Palatine, which made him responsible for designing pageants and other festivities of the court. As a servant of the court, his duties also included discovering antiques, curious items, and freakish animals for the collection of the Hapsburg dynasty.

An entertaining artist, Arcimboldo enjoyed immense popularity during his lifetime. He constructed fantastic heads from masses of fruits and vegetables to produce double images. For example, in the painting *Allegory of Summer* (1563), what appears to be a nose in a profile portrait is really a warty cucumber. In the same portrait, the cheek of the figure is really an apple combined with other fruits and vegetables on a platter. A double image is one that either shows the head and shoulders of a person or just a pile of fruit, depending on how one views the piece. An ingenious individual who employed wit in his portraits, Arcimboldo was a visual Aesop (a sixth century B.C. Greek author of fables), creating morals, such as the double image of a human forehead and a wolf, which implies that each is a symbol of cunningness.

His work observed analogies that were apparent and popular in his day and thought of as a science. He was regarded not as an eccentric, but merely as a brilliant man who had the ability to express humor and wit in art.

The Renaissance placed emphasis on the development of the individual and allowed women the freedom to expand their positions and seek careers outside the domestic realm.

Sofonisba Anguissola was the eldest of six girls and one boy born to the nobleman Amilcare Anguissola (1494–1573) in the northern town of Cremona in Italy. Her father subscribed to the theory that a proper education should include Latin, music, and painting, so all his children were trained in the three disciplines. Anguissola was one of the few artists in the history of western art to come from nobility. From 1546–1549, she studied with Bernardino Campi, a local portrait artist, who trained her so well that she was able to teach her younger sisters the craft. Her first known work is *Self Portrait* (1554). Her study set a precedent in encouraging other Italian painters to accept female students. Her most popular work was *Boy Pinched by a Crayfish* (1560), which her father sent to the artist Michelangelo (see no. 11). Michelangelo responded by sending Anguissola some of his own drawings for her to reproduce.

Anguissola was a prolific painter, and more than fifty signed works attributed to her survive. Like most women of her time, she specialized in portraiture. She painted a number of self-portraits because images of her were in demand; each varied in size and format. She sometimes depicted herself as a religious image; other times she was playing an instrument or reading a book in order to illustrate that she had an education and was proficient in other arts and learning. While still in her twenties, she was sufficiently well known to be invited to join the court of Philip II of Spain. She arrived in 1560 and stayed for ten years, first as a lady-in-waiting to the queen, then as official court painter to the king. While in Spain, her fame was so great that Pope Pius IV asked her to send him a portrait of the queen.

She later married a Sicilian lord, Fabrizio de Moncada, and moved with him to Palermo, Sicily, but he died four years later.

The remainder of her long life was then divided between Genoa and Palermo. In Genoa, she was visited by the artist Anthony van Dyck (see no. 24) in 1624, to whom she gave artistic advice. He said she had a "good memory and a sharp mind." She was the first woman artist to achieve international fame and the first by whom a large body of work still exists. Her work exemplified a straightforward realism, creating a sense of conversation in her pictures. Her paintings had an expressive quality that made her subjects come alive, only "lacking in speech," as wrote the author Giorgio Vassari in his book *Lives of the Painters, Sculptors, and Architects*.

Sofonisba Anguissola

19. EL GRECO
(1541–1614)

A prosperous man who received members of the nobility and intellectual elite into his home, Domenico Theotocopuli was a popular entertainer and socialite, as well as a painter. He was given the nickname El Greco (el-GRECK-o) by the Spanish. It means "the Greek," in reference to his birthplace in Crete. The Spanish thought of El Greco as a foreigner in Spain, even though he glorified the country in his art. All his life he signed his work with his real name in Greek letters.

At twenty-five years of age, El Greco went to Venice, Italy, and was employed in the workshop of Titian (1487?–1576), remaining there for eleven years. He then moved to Toledo, Spain, to begin his first commission from the Church of Santo Domingo, which marked the turning point of his career. His first piece was the *Assumption of the Virgin* (1577), demonstrating his move toward unconventional colors, distorted groupings of figures, and elongated proportions of the body. His work is defined by disorder of composition of the body and ecstatic expressions and gestures in dazzling colors. It is presumed that he emigrated to Spain because he was ostracized by the art community in Italy, after suggesting that Michelangelo's (see no. 11) *Last Judgment* in the Sistine Chapel should be torn down and that he could repaint it.

El Greco did not emulate the religious painting style of Spain and was considered a rebel and eccentric by the standards of the land. His unconventional domestic life also made him an outsider in religious Spain, which did not condone two people living together and having children out of wedlock. His fees were extraordinarily high, and several documents exist in his name pertaining to litigation over payments where he took his patrons to court for refusing to pay his price. In 1586, he painted one of his greatest masterpieces, *The Burial of Count Orgaz*, which portrays the funeral of a fourteenth century nobleman whose soul is rising to a heaven populated with angels and contemporary political figures. The work is indicative of his style of elongated human forms and his technique of horror vacui, or fear of unfilled spaces.

El Greco

Spain was regarded as a declining society compared with Italy, yet El Greco settled there for thirty-seven years to become the first of Spain's triumvirate of great artists, including Diego Velazquez (see no. 25) and Francisco de Goya (see no. 33).

It was difficult for El Greco to live in a country where the government controlled all freedoms, especially during the Inquisition, when Spain attempted to rid itself of its undesired citizens. The fact that he held a respected position kept him secure in that dangerous time.

Lavinia Fontana, an example of women artists who emerged from Bologna, Italy, received much of her education from the foreign artists, architects, and scholars who visited her father, Prospero Fontana, a successful painter of the time. The city of Bologna took on an exceptionally progressive attitude toward its female citizens, which encouraged women to seek professions in many fields.

Fontana was taught to paint by her father and gained fame as a portrait painter at a young age. The fashionable ladies of Bologna admired her talent to depict the truth in a flattering manner, with special detail paid to their jewels and adornments.

The minute attention paid to elaborate costumes is best demonstrated in her famous *Portrait of a Lady with a Lap Dog* (1580). The background she employed when depicting women was plain, while her portraits of men incorporated backgrounds that alluded to their professions.

She received her first authoritative commission in 1572 from Pope Gregory XIII and was summoned to Rome at the height of her growing reputation. An oversize portrait she made of the *Stoning of St. Stephen* (1603?) for the altarpiece of the church of St. Paul was not successful. Women were prohibited from using nude models, and Fontana found it difficult to represent the musculature of the male body without one.

However, Fontana was in great demand in Rome as a portrait painter. She was elected to the Roman Academy, a rare honor for a woman, and this allowed her to charge a large fee for her work.

Fontana received many marriage proposals, yet she was hesitant because she did not want to disrupt her career. She said that she "would never take a husband unless he were willing to leave her the mistress of her beloved art." She eventually married in 1577, to Gian Paolo

Lavinia Fontana

Zappi, who studied at her father's studio but was considered untalented. In what was a role reversal for an Italian couple of the time, her husband took over the household while she continued with her career.

Lavinia Fontana expanded the role of women as artists by taking commissions to do altarpieces and religious paintings for churches. Shortly before her death, a medal was struck in her honor, one side showing her in profile as a gentlewoman, the other side showing an artist at work in a frenzy with hair in disarray. At least 135 works have been attributed to Fontana, proving her to be a productive artist. No female artist before her enjoyed the success she did. It was said that when she passed the Lord of Sora and Vignola at the Roman Academy, he rose to meet her, an honor usually bestowed only upon royalty.

Caravaggio

Michelangelo Merisi da Caravaggio (cahr-a-VODGE-o) obtained his surname from the town of his birth. He was an Italian painter whose life was as dark, colorful, and violent as his paintings. Although his father, Fermo Merisi, was a master mason and architect, Caravaggio was apprenticed at the age of ten to a painter near Milan, Italy. By age seventeen, he left for Rome, where he turned from the prevalent taste for the classics to using everyday common people as models for his paintings of mythological figures and saints.

While interested in naturalistic painting, he could not afford models, so he began to paint mirror images of himself. His aim was to paint the human figure in its exact replica. The moods in his pictures vary from mischief to anguish. He used his own face on the portrait of *Medusa* (1594), with an expression of comedy in the figure.

He was discovered at age twenty-seven by Cardinal del Monte. The cardinal allowed Caravaggio to paint the way he preferred and gave him housing. The cardinal was instrumental in obtaining Caravaggio's first great commission, the three *St. Matthew* paintings for the Contarelli Chapel.

Caravaggio had an inclination for low-class environments and was constantly humanizing holy and miraculous figures into common form. He rendered realistic interpretations of religious scenes and biblical characters by disregarding reverential poses and using contrasts of light and shade to bring the figures to the forefront of the painting so that they could not be ignored. He painted the *St. Matthew* figure as a stocky man—a simple rough peasant sitting with crossed legs and bare feet with a female angel at his side. He was forced to redo his work, depicting the saint with the usual spiritual reverence. Caravaggio intended his art for common people; however, these people were the ones most offended by it. Common people were conditioned to believe that reverence for saints had to be glorious. Instead, his patrons were cultivated men who felt elevated at seeing saints depicted as ordinary men.

Caravaggio was an angry young man, prone to street fights. From 1600 to 1606, he is mentioned in police records for wounding a captain, assaulting a waiter by throwing an artichoke at him, throwing stones at the police, insulting a corporal, and more.

After a brawl over money he lost in a game, Caravaggio killed his opponent, then fled to Naples, Italy, to await a pardon from the Pope.

Caravaggio visited Malta, where he was received with honor into the Order of Malta as a cavalier, but he quarreled with one of his superiors and was jailed.

In 1610, Caravaggio received a pardon from the Pope and set off for Rome, but he was mistakenly arrested and detained, thus missing his boat, where all his belongings and paintings were stored. In despair after his release, he began to run in the direction of the departed ship and collapsed, dying a few days later of malignant fever.

Peter Paul Rubens, a Flemish painter whose style became internationally famous, made a lasting impression on many artists, including Jean Antoine Watteau (see no. 28) in the eighteenth century and Auguste Renoir (see no. 52) in the nineteenth century. Rubens was born at Siegen, Westphalia (now Germany). His father, Jan Rubens, a prominent lawyer, had converted from Catholicism to Calvinism and was forced to leave Antwerp, Belgium, with his family due to religious persecution. In 1587, after the death of his father, Rubens and his family returned to Antwerp, where he began to study the classics in a Latin school. Not yet fifteen years old, he became a court page to Lady Margaret of Ligne. He then decided to become a painter, although painting was considered a less respectable profession. He attained the rank of master painter of the Antwerp painters' guild at the age of twenty-one. Described as a precocious painter because of his bold brush stroke and luminous color, Rubens created vibrant art, involving the tension between the intellect and the emotion, the classical and the romantic.

He left Antwerp in 1600 for Italy, where he was employed by the Duke of Mantua, Vincenzo Gonzaga. He stayed with the duke for nine years, also serving as the duke's emissary to King Philip III of Spain. His time with the duke gave him the financial means to travel and study the works of Michelangelo (see no. 11) and Caravaggio (see no. 21).

After formulating the first innovative expressions of the Baroque style in Italy, Rubens returned to Antwerp and was employed by the burgomaster, or mayor. His major works of this time were *Elevation of the Cross* (1610) and *Descent from the Cross* (1614), demonstrating realism and dynamic movement, which were typical of his style.

The demand for his work was so great that Rubens established an enormous workshop in which he completed the initial sketches and final touches, but his apprentices did all the intermediary steps. He kept meticulous records and was very explicit as to how much of a particular painting was executed by his own hand.

In 1622, Rubens visited Paris and was commissioned by King Louis XIII to do a series of paintings. At the same time, Rubens was a special agent in peace negotiations among the Netherlands and the countries of Spain, England, and France. His contemporaries thought of him first as a diplomat and then as a painter, as he performed international negotiations at the highest level and was entrusted with state secrets. In painting, Rubens is best represented by *The Judgment of Paris* (1637). In this work, voluptuous goddesses pose against a green landscape, both elements representing the greatness of creation. This painting culminated Rubens' lifelong concern to paint what he considered to be the most beautiful things in the world.

Peter Paul Rubens

Artemisia Gentileschi was said to have advanced the development of the style of Caravaggio (see no. 21), which was characterized by theatrical depictions of the human figure and the humanization of spiritual and holy entities. Her importance to Italian art in this style was second only to that of Caravaggio himself.

Gentileschi was the first child of Orazio Gentileschi, who was a court painter to King Charles I of England. She was known more for the scandal in her life, rather than her contributions to the Baroque style of art in Italy. In 1612, Gentileschi's father accused his friend and colleague Agostino Tassi, hired to teach Artemisia perspective in art, of assaulting his daughter. A trial ensued and she was subjected to torture by thumbscrews—used as a kind of lie-detector test—before a court of law to assess the validity of her testimony. The trial was a source of gossip for the public and did nothing

Artemisia Gentileschi

to harm Tassi's reputation, even though he was found guilty of the crime.

Gentileschi married Pietro Antonio de Vincenzo Stiattesi a month after the trial, and they settled in Florence, where she enrolled in the Academia del Disegno. At twenty-three years of age, she was made a member of the Florence Academy.

From the beginning of her career, she concentrated on full-scale compositions of figures. An early painting of hers is *Judith with her Maidservant* (1611), which reflects a popular Old Testament theme in Baroque art. Gentileschi frequently depicted this scene as a reflection of the assault she suffered and the humiliation she underwent as a result of her trial. Her work expressed vigorous realism, while the poses of her figures stressed the psychological drama of the scene, rather than the physical charm of the female subject. In 1638, she joined her father in England at the court of Charles I and assisted in painting nine canvases that were set into the ceiling of the Queen's House in Greenwich.

During the Baroque period, female painters were prominent, and Artemisia Gentileschi was the most remarkable. Her power of expression and her dramatic intensity, usually thought of as male characteristics, surpassed most of her contemporaries. Other aspects of her life, such as the affairs she was supposed to have had with a variety of men, added to her scandalous reputation.

The women she portrayed in her paintings reflect a basic hostility toward men. A recurrent theme in her work is the female heroine as a powerful and sensuous person. As an early feminist, Gentileschi revealed the subject from the female perspective. Her work was also unique in the approaches she used, such as stopping the action at the climax of the event rather than after the action has occurred.

24. SIR ANTHONY VAN DYCK
(1599–1641)

Anthony van Dyck (van-DYKE), the son of a rich silk merchant, was apprenticed to the Flemish historical painter Hendrik van Balen at age eleven. He became a professional artist with a private studio and pupils at age sixteen. By the time he was nineteen, van Dyck was considered one of the most brilliant colorists in the history of art, and he was admitted into the St. Luke guild of painters in Antwerp, Belgium, the place of his birth. A week after his twenty-first birthday, van Dyck was signed on as a chief assistant to Peter Paul Rubens (see no. 22) in a contract to decorate the Church of St. Charles Borromeo.

After its completion, van Dyck left for Italy, where he remained for six years. He was in great demand as a portraitist, due to his developed mix of colors, unsurpassed by any other artist. The Romans dubbed him the "knightly painter" because he demanded

Sir Anthony Van Dyck

equality between himself and his patrons. Van Dyck considered himself a painter only and rejected the notion of the artist as a super craftsman or an exceptional person whose gifts made him or her acceptable in society.

In 1632, van Dyck settled in London, where his reputation for creating incredible likenesses of the English aristocracy earned him a position as chief court painter to King Charles I of England. He was later made a knight of the court. He received a town house and an annual pension above the payments he received for executing portraits of the king and queen. By virtue of his popularity and the number of portraits he was commissioned to do, van Dyck was forced to hire assistants to

paint everything but the faces in portraits. Van Dyck was unique as a painter for his style of adding tension to the visual likeness. Each portrait depicts fine-boned, slender figures with full lips and curly hair, as if all the subjects descended from the same lineage.

In 1635, he painted his masterpiece, *Charles I in Hunting Dress*, a standing figure representing the haughty grace of the monarch. He established new styles in Flemish art and founded the English school of painting, which gave him artistic heirs such as Sir Joshua Reynolds (see no. 31) and Thomas Gainsborough (see no. 32). In 1640, he returned to Antwerp, Belgium, where he was made dean of the painters' guild. He died in England a year later.

Along with El Greco (see no. 19) and Francisco de Goya (see no. 33), Diego de Silva y Velazquez (ve-LAHSS-kez) forms the triumvirate of famous Spanish painters. Velazquez was born in Seville, Spain, in 1599, the oldest of six children, to parents of minor nobility.

His first instruction in art came from Francesco Pacheco, whose daughter he later married. As a painter, Velazquez recorded the world around him directly as he saw it—without false illusions of beauty or grandeur. He took an interest in realistic subject matter, portraits, and religious scenes, which characterize his work between 1617 and 1623. The most famous painting of this period is the *Water Seller of Seville* (1620). Here, the effect of light and shadow combines with the direct observation of nature, and the work is compared to that of Caravaggio (see no. 21). Velazquez's religious works incorporate models drawn from the streets of Seville or from his own circle of friends. In the picture *Adoration of the Magi* (1619), he painted his family in the guise of biblical figures.

At age twenty-two, he made his first trip to Madrid to search for a position as a court painter, returning without success. But leaving again a year later, he executed a portrait of the king and was named official painter and courtier to King Philip IV of Spain. At that point in his career, mythological subjects occupied his time, although he always maintained his style of realism. An example of this is in the portrait of the wine god *Bacchus* (1629), where the god is portrayed drinking with ordinary men in an open field.

Velazquez was said to be a socially conscious man who had a desire to be a noble. He felt that to be a companion to the king was as outstanding a prize as being a famous painter. While in service to Philip IV, Velazquez had the opportunity to meet with the painter Peter Paul Rubens (see no. 22). He was also inspired to visit Italy and travel through its cities. While in Italy, he produced his notable *Joseph's Blood-Stained Coat Brought to Jacob* (1630), which combines the chiaroscuro style of using light-and-shadow techniques to create drama. Velazquez returned to Spain in the 1630s and resumed his duties as court portraitist, producing a series of equestrian portraits of the king and queen and the heir Don Baltasar.

Attacked by critics for his "tasteless embracing of low subject matter," Velazquez was a realist who was frank and intimate in his paintings. In the work *Surrender of Breda* (1635), Velazquez portrays a heroic action incorporating human sympathy. The scene presents inattentive troops and a horse whose back is turned to the surrender and in fact is lifting its leg in a gesture of impudence; the battlefield smokes in the distance, while the attention is focused on the meeting of the two generals, creating a feeling of closeness between the observer and the subject.

Diego Velazquez

26. REMBRANDT
(1606–1669)

Born in Leiden, Netherlands, Rembrandt van Rijn, a Dutch baroque artist, ranks as one of the greatest painters in the history of Western art. The son of a miller, his parents had high ambitions for him, and at the age fourteen, they enrolled him at the University of Leiden. But Rembrandt dropped out that same year and apprenticed at the studio of Jacob van Swanenburgh. At age seventeen, he went to Amsterdam, Netherlands, and studied with the historical painter Pieter Lastman. After six months, he had mastered all he had been taught and returned to Leiden to establish himself as an independent painter. This period marks his style of dramatic subjects, crowded arrangements, and contrasts of light and shadow.

When Rembrandt was twenty-five, he returned to Amsterdam and remained there. Rembrandt created over six hundred paintings, of which roughly sixty were self-portraits. His early paintings, such as the *Portrait of a Man and His Wife* (1633), demonstrate his preoccupation with the features of the figure and the details of clothing and furniture.

No other artist subjected himself to the scrutiny and self-analysis that Rembrandt lent himself. He never attempted to hide his homely features, although deep shadows cover his face in many portraits. The self-portraits of this style may have been done to show his finesse of chiaroscuro (the dramatic employment of light and darkness) to invoke emotion. Biblical subjects account for one-third of Rembrandt's works. He used the flamboyant baroque style to express a sense of drama, which was unusual for Protestant Holland in the seventeenth century, where religious works were not highly regarded.

Rembrandt's first major public commission in Amsterdam was *The Anatomy Lesson of Dr. Tulp* (1632). The piece depicts the regents of the Guild of Surgeons assembled for a dissection and lecture. Rembrandt used a pyramid

Rembrandt

arrangement of the figures, creating a natural balance.

In 1641, Rembrandt was commissioned for the group portrait *The Company of Captain Frans Banning Cocq*, the actual title for the work that is generally referred to as *The Night Watch*. The painting, which is 12-feet- (3.7-m-) high and 14-feet- (4.3-m-) long, depicts the organization of the civil guard. Rembrandt had dramatized an imaginary scene where the civil guard was called to arms. He introduced figures for the sake of composition and placed several members in shadows while vividly illuminating others.

Despite his success as an artist, teacher, and art dealer, Rembrandt's luxurious life-style forced him to declare bankruptcy in 1656. His production of paintings, however, did not decline. He continued to work, producing *Jacob Blessing the Sons of Joseph* (1656) and a self-portrait, *Portrait of the Painter in Old Age* (1659?), where he depicts himself in a sarcastic mood.

Elisabetta Sirani

Displaying an early artistic talent, Elisabetta Sirani, born in Bolgna, Italy, began studying art under her father, the painter Giovanni Andrea Sirani. A family friend, the Count Cesare Malvasia, noticed Sirani's abilities and persuaded her father to take her on as a pupil. Her early education also included Bible study, Greek and Roman mythology, harp, and voice. Despite her passion for art, she did not allow it to interfere with her home duties. Elisabetta's artistic success made her family financially dependent on her commissions and fees from art lessons.

Some believe that her father was a tyrant and prevented her from marrying for fear of losing her financial support. Others believe Sirani chose to remain single for the sake of her art.

She painted portraits, religious works, allegorical themes, and, occasionally, stories from ancient history. Her style is characterized by the sentimentality of the subject. Extremely particular about the distinct facial expressions of her subjects, she used deep colors and shadowed eye sockets to suggest depth of feeling. Although her art idealized the features of the subjects, it also reflected the inadequacy of training allotted to women because they were prohibited from studying nude figures.

Sirani worked with such incredible speed and was so productive that she was accused of having others paint the portraits. One hundred and fifty paintings have been substantiated as Sirani originals. Her speed was said to have been attributed to the pressure of her father. To prove her abilities, on May 13, 1664, she invited a group of distinguished persons to view her paint a portrait of Prince Leopold of Tuscany, which she completed in one sitting.

An important teacher, she established a painting school for women and taught her sister Anna Maria (1645-1715) to paint. Anna Maria also became a professional artist.

At the young age of twenty-seven, Sirani died of suspicious causes. Sirani's father accused the maid of killing her, but the maid was acquitted after a lengthy trial. Sirani was given a large funeral by Bologna's prominent citizens. An enormous domed catafalque (a temporary structure representing a tomb placed over the coffin) was made for the occasion, in which a life-sized sculpture of Sirani at her easel was placed.

Regarded as a forerunner of nineteenth-century impressionism, Jean-Antoine Watteau (wat-TOE) was born in Valenciennes, a Flemish town that had come under French possession. The second son of a master roofer, he lived in a region ravaged by recurrent warfare, and with a father who exhibited violent behavior and did not approve of his son's ambition to become an artist. At age fourteen, Watteau began to study painting under the tutelage of an obscure local painter specializing in religious subjects.

By the time he was eighteen, Watteau was disowned by his family for his continual pursuit of an artistic career. He went to Paris, where he found a job copying paintings of saints in exact replica for a merchant who sold souvenir religious paintings. To alleviate his boredom at work, Watteau would sketch the variety of beggars, peddlers, and tradespeople around the market place.

After two years, he became an apprentice to Claude Gillot, a painter of theatrical scenes. Gillot influenced Watteau's interest in the theater, which was to become the main subject of his work. At age twenty-four, he became an assistant to the decorator Claude Audran. Audran was also the curator of the Luxemburg palace, which held a collection of paintings by Peter Paul Rubens (see no. 22). Watteau studied the works of Rubens, whose use of rich colors influenced Watteau's style. Studying the series of Rubens's paintings inspired Watteau to compete in the art contest Prix de Rome. His entry failed to win, and he returned to his home town for a while and painted the soldiers there.

Watteau returned to Paris soon after and won official recognition with admission into the French Academy, a government-sponsored institution for artists, with the painting *Embarkation for Cythera* (1717). This work shows a garden scene where couples walk

Jean-Antoine Watteau

towards a boat, and it is symbolic of having taken a journey to an ideal world that must be left behind. The figures in the painting were most probably friends of his, dressed in costumes, whom he used as models and superimposed onto backgrounds painted from nature. Watteau's genius was his use of body language in his work. The painting was the beginning of his style labeled as fete gallantes. The term refers to his common theme of yearning for simpler times and his creation of surroundings with figures that didn't belong there.

Shortly before his death from tuberculosis, Watteau painted *Christ on the Cross* (1721?). It reflected his concern at the time about life after death. Later, a friend, Jean de Julienne, compiled Watteau's works into a book entitled *Recueil Julienne*. The compilation brought Watteau to a larger audience than he ever had while he was living.

A London-born painter and engraver who satirized the follies of his age, William Hogarth, the son of a school teacher, was apprenticed to a silversmith at the age of fifteen. There he learned how to make coats of arms, family crests, design plates for booksellers, and more. At the age of twenty-three, he established himself as an independent engraver and also illustrated books. He first became known in 1726 for his illustrations for the satirical poem *Hudibras* (1726), by fellow Englishman Samuel Butler.

At the same time, Hogarth enrolled at St. Martin's Academy to learn the basics of painting and drawing. He detested the manner and style professed by the school's director, Sir James Thornhill, and did not apply it to his work.

Hogarth began painting portraits, gods, and heroes at age thirty-one. He had little success at it and turned to painting occurrences of everyday life in London. He used publicized scandals of the day as his inspiration and became known as a social critic using pictures instead of words.

William Hogarth

Hogarth's first work was a series of six paintings engraved in a book, *A Harlot's Progress* (1732). Along with some text written by Hogarth, the book contained detailed paintings of furniture and clothing and told the story of a country girl who ventures to the city and the adventures she encounters. Falling in with bad company, the country girl finally dies in poverty, a fitting end for what Hogarth termed "the modern moral subject." The book was immediately popular and was followed by *A Rake's Progress (1735)*, a narrative of eight pictures. This work followed a foolish young man through a career of gambling, carousing, bankruptcy, imprisonment for debt, marriage for money, and more. Although virtue was not always rewarded in Hogarth's scenes, vice was always punished.

Hogarth is renowned for his satires of marriage for money and his opinions on social values of the upper class. Hogarth hoped to bring about social reform by depicting the ills of society. His work was often plagiarized, which led him to assist in the passage of copyright laws in 1735 that later became known as Hogarth's Act.

Never compromising in his factual accounts of life, he once painted a historical piece showing soldiers drinking and acting foolish. Hogarth gained permission to present the painting to King George II, who was angered by the work.

Hogarth's career began to decline. He attempted to regain favor by publishing his aesthetic principles of art titled *The Analysis of Beauty* (1753). This book details his analytical approach for organizing the subjects in his paintings. The book was criticized as being dull. During the last five years of his life, Hogarth was engaged in political feuds with the British political reformer John Wilkes (1727–1797), whom he had often satirized in engravings.

30. CANALETTO
(1697–1768)

Born in Venice, Italy, Giovanni Antonio Canal, known as Canaletto, was renowned for his vedute, or views, of the city. Canaletto received his instruction in painting and perspective from his father, Bernardo Canal, who was a painter of theatrical scenery. After a trip to Rome when he was twenty-two years old, Canaletto became heavily influenced by landscape painters, especially Giovanni Paolo Panini, and established himself as a painter of landscapes and city views. At the time, city views were relatively new and rare in art. Returning to Venice soon after, he was influenced by the artist Luce Carlevaris and began to depict views that were topographically accurate and unique in the precise rendering of architectural structures.

Canaletto's work is marked by strong contrasts of light and shade to depict the drama of the landscape. This is most evident in his painting *Stone Mason's Yard* (1730). In his works, he used luminous light combined with glowing color in delicate detail to depict a storm developing in the sky, such as in *Piazza San Marco* (1740). His principal patrons were English aristocrats, for whom the scenes of the city and its festivals, such as the annual celebration of the Marriage of Venice to the Sea, were pretty souvenirs to take back to their homes. Success came quickly, and he soon met Joseph Smith, a merchant, art collector, and British consul at Venice, who later became his agent.

When the War of the Austrian Succession interrupted travel, Canaletto lost his main patronage and moved to England in 1746; except for a few visits to Venice, he remained there until 1755. There he painted English landscapes, such as the River Thames, and various country houses. While Canaletto was in England, critics said that his style had become too linear and mechanical in repetition of

Canaletto

familiar themes. His popularity did not waiver in spite of the criticism. Canaletto returned to Venice in 1755 and began producing capriccii—imaginary scenes that incorporated actual architectural subjects from a variety of places. Extremely popular, he was imitated in style during his lifetime in both Italy and England. Canaletto's agent sold the majority of his works to King George III (1738–1820) of England. Upon Canaletto's death, his nephew, Bernardo Bellotto, adopted his style and brought it to Central Europe. Artistic followers of his style in England included William Marlow and Samuel Scott.

31. SIR JOSHUA REYNOLDS
(1723–1792)

Sir Joshua Reynolds

The son of a clergyman, Sir Joshua Reynolds was the first English painter to achieve social recognition for his artistic achievements. Born in Plympton, Devonshire, Reynolds first learned portraiture from the painter Thomas Hudson in London. At the time, portraiture offered stability and respect.

In 1749, he sailed to the Mediterranean and spent three years traveling in Italy, where he worked at becoming a gentleman and improved as an artist. While in Italy, he was heavily influenced by the use of warm colors and clarity he viewed in the work of the Italian painter Tintoretto (see no. 16).

Reynolds was a shrewd man who considered art to be a business and adopted social pretenses to align himself with the aristocracy. He became an elitist and snob and tried to distance himself from his humble beginning. He is credited with over two thousand portraits which epitomized London society of his day.

The portraits by Reynolds are distinguished by a serene dignity of the subject, allusions to classical figures in history, vibrant color, and realistic portrayal of character combined with a keen understanding of human nature.

In England in 1764, Reynolds founded the Literary Club, which included essayist Samuel Johnson (1709–1784), actor David Garrick (1717–1779), and statesman Edmund Burke (1729–1797), to name a few. When the Royal Academy of Arts was instituted in 1768, Reynolds was elected president, later made a knight, and given an honorary degree from Oxford College. This represented a step forward in the way in which society treated and viewed artist.

A year later, Reynolds delivered his first discourse to the students of the academy on the idealistic principles of academic art, entitled *Discourses*, which also stressed the importance of grandeur in art and rigid academic training. At the same time, he exhibited his greatest portrait, *The Tragic Muse* (1784), for which the English actress Sarah Siddons (1755–1831) was the subject. Other of his famous works include *Honorable Augustus Keppel* (1754), *William Robertson* (1772), and *Duchess of Devonshire and her Daughter* (1786), which demonstrates the use of a subtle brush stroke to invoke a sense of dignity.

32. Thomas Gainsborough
(1727–1788)

The youngest of nine children born to a cloth merchant in Sudbury, Suffolk, England, landscape painter and portraitist Thomas Gainsborough demonstrated a talent for drawing at an early age. At age fourteen, he went to London, where he studied etching under Hugh Gravelot and painting under Francis Haymon at the St. Martin Academy.

Returning to his home in 1746, he married Margaret Burr, who was sixteen, and began to paint "conversational piece" portraits. These were intimate paintings that included landscapes of the English countryside. The works showed the influence of seventeenth-century Dutch landscape painting, especially that of Jacob van Ruisdael.

Six years later, he moved to Ipswich and built up his practice. In order to find more subjects and make money, he later moved to the more prosperous city of Bath. In Bath, he concentrated on the full-scale portrait and was influenced by the works of Anthony van Dyck (see no. 24) and the rich colors of Peter Paul Rubens (see no. 22). The painting *Mr. William Poyntz* (1762) even depicts men dressed in clothing similar to that worn by van Dyck's subjects.

While in Bath, Gainsborough occasionally exhibited his work at the Society of Artists in London. He became well known and was invited to be among the original members of the Royal Academy of Arts in London, established by King George III in 1768.

By 1774, Gainsborough was extremely prosperous and moved to London, where he remained for the rest of his life. It is speculated that he moved there to compete with Sir Joshua Reynolds (see no. 31) for portrait commissions. In contrast to Reynolds, Gainsborough was described as a spontaneous

Thomas Gainsborough

painter, whose subjects did not appear rigid, and "a master at handling paint." His most famous piece is *Blue Boy* (1779), notable for its cool blue colors, as opposed to the reds used by Reynolds.

By 1780, he had gained the favor of King George III and painted many portraits of the royal court. At this time, he also began to paint in another manner, which he called "fancy pictures," characterized by darker landscapes and imaginative figures that dominated the paintings. The best known is the *Country Girl with Dog and Pitcher* (1785).

Gainsborough left no immediate heirs to his artistic style, but his style later influenced artists Richard Westall (1765–1836) and Thomas Barker (1813–1882).

Francisco de Goya

The son of a painter and guilder of altar-pieces, Francisco José de Goya was born in the small town of Fuendetodos, Spain. He began his formal artistic training at age fourteen, apprenticing with a local painting master, José Luzán (1710–1785). Goya's acceptance into the art world came in 1771, when he won second place in a painting competition in Parma, Italy, representing Hannibal the Conqueror looking down on Italy from the Alps.

Returning to Spain, he met the painter Francisco Bayeu (1734–1795), who influenced his early baroque style. He later married Bayeu's sister. Goya's first commission in Spain was in 1774 with forty-three cartoons, illustrating the life of the people at that time, for the tapestries for the Royal Factory of Santa Barbara. One famous cartoon from the tapestry was *The Crockery Vendor*, noted for its realism and vivid human characterization.

By the time he was thirty-nine years old, Goya had became an official painter to King Charles III (1716–1788) of Spain. It was at this time that he broke with Bayeu and adopt-ed the techniques of Diego Velazquez (see no. 25). The *Duke of Osuna* (1785) typifies his change of style, featuring luminous backgrounds and stark simplicity in the subject.

In 1792, Goya became ill and was left almost completely deaf. The episode turned Goya's work from quaint to tragic and analytical, based on his observations of everyday life. His work was then characterized by bold and swift brush strokes and colors of gray, black, brown, and touches of red.

Goya's celebrated work, showing his mockery of corruption in the aristocracy, is a set of eighty etchings titled *Los Caprichos* (1794–1798). The city life motif, emphasizing satire and parody, reflected his conception of a society held together by a loose structure of conventions that were ready to snap. His popularity grew, and in 1795, he was elected president of the Royal Academy, a government sponsored art institute. Four years later, he was named First Painter to the king.

In 1808, Spain underwent a political crisis as Napolean tried to impose his sovereignty. Goya witnessed the horrors of warfare. He created a series of paintings known as *Disasters of War* (1808–1814), using political allegory to portray the degradation of man killing man. One noted work from the series, *The Second of May 1808* (1814), depicts an uprising in the street in which citizens armed with sticks attack soldiers.

Goya also created the series known as *Los Proverbios* or *The Follies* (1813–1818). These paintings are marked by dark moods that reveal a world of nightmares. In *Saturn Devouring His Children* (1820), rapid, expressionist brush strokes, showing contrast of light and shade, are evident.

In 1824, Goya settled in France, where his work softened in tone and color. One such painting from this period is called the *Milkmaid of Bordeaux* (1827).

A celebrated artist in her own time, Elisabeth Louise Vigée-Lebrun developed an interest in drawing during her years in boarding school, which she attended from the ages of six to eleven. Born to the painter Louis Vigée in Paris on April 16, 1755, she received drawing and painting lessons from Gabriel Doyen and from others who visited her father's studio when she was home during her holiday visits.

At the young age of twelve, she began a professional career and supported her mother after her father died in 1767. Her wit and beauty attracted patrons as much as her talent did.

Remarkable as a portrait painter, she painted in oils and depicted the personalities of her clients in her work, and she was always inventive with poses and settings. Her paintings would exaggerate the charms of her subjects and gloss over their imperfections. Among her patrons were Count Schouvaloff of Russia, whom Vigée-Lebrun painted in exact detail wearing a fur-edged jacket adorned with two decorations. He also wore bands of silk ribbons across his waist to mark other honors. Lebrun shows his body turned to the left while he looks out to the right. The averted gaze was meant to give him an aura of reserve indicative of the aristocratic class.

At age twenty, she hesitantly married the art dealer and painter Jean-Baptise Pierre Lebrun. He took her money and insisted she give art lessons to supplement her income. Yet he was also well connected in the art world and introduced her to upper class people and exposed her to prominent art.

Her fame was soon acclaimed by royal members of the court. In 1779, she was called on to paint Queen Marie Antoinette, after which she was named the official painter to the queen and completed twenty portraits of her. The most famous was *Marie-Antoinette and Her Children* (1787). The Queen facilitated her acceptance into the Academie Royale, a government sponsored art institute. Another famous piece was the *Portrait of the Marquise de Jaucourt* (1789).

Due to her close relationship with the Queen, Vigée-Lebrun was forced to escape Paris during the French Revolution in 1789. Leaving her husband, she lived in exile in Europe for twelve years. She had already established an international reputation and continued to paint.

Before her death, she wrote an account of her life and of European society in the late eighteenth and early nineteenth century. Entitled *Souvenirs,* the book was first published in 1835.

Elisabeth Lebrun

35. WILLIAM BLAKE
(1757–1827)

English poet, engraver, and painter William Blake was born on November 28, 1757, in London, to a father who sold stockings. When he was four years old, Blake stated that he had seen a vision of God. This visionary power remained his source of inspiration throughout his artistic career.

A nervous child and sensitive to punishment, Blake only went to school until the age of ten, then entered the drawing school of Henry Pars. His parents purchased prints of famous artworks for him to copy.

By the time he was fourteen, he was apprenticed to the engraver James Basire (1730–1802). After completing his seven-year term, he studied at the Royal Academy, but he rebelled against the doctrine of its president Sir Joshua Reynolds (see no. 31). Blake believed in intuition and a trust in the imagination when creating art, and he did not want to follow an academic system. At twenty-five years of age, he married Catherine Boucher. Two years later, he set up a print shop that failed after a few years. He then returned to engraving and illustrating.

The death of his brother, Robert, in 1787, brought a new mysticism to Blake's life. It was at this time that he developed a technique of illuminated printing, an elaborate combination of engraving and hand-tinting, which allowed him to fuse art and poetry. Although the technique is not completely understood, it is believed he drew on copper plates the pictures for the poems he wrote, using a liquid impervious to acid. He then applied acid to burn away the rest of the plate, leaving the words and pictures in relief. The work was then given a color wash and later finished by hand in water color. He used this technique to publish his *Songs of Innocence* (1789) and *Songs of Experience* (1794). The theme of these books was the struggle between reason and imagination.

Blake's paintings focused on religious subjects, the most famous being illustrations of the *Book of Job* (1825). Blake's style was a precursor to modern art. The use of rigid geometric patterns and the emphasis on line and color as a means of expression were inspirational in a time that favored realism in art. Other works include *Marriage of Heaven and Hell* (1793) and *Milton* (1810?).

Constant quarrels and a refusal to subjugate himself and conform to his patrons' desires lost him many commissions, and he was left poor and depressed. In an attempt to earn money and raise his reputation, he held his own art exhibition, charging an entrance fee and advertising the event with the motto "Fit audience find tho' few." The stunt met with bad reviews, and he failed to achieve his goals.

William Blake

Regarded as America's first major land-scapist, Washington Allston introduced to the United States the art movement known as romanticism. Romanticism emphasized nature and atmosphere, arising in opposition to classical formalism and rationalism. He was born in Georgetown County, South Carolina. Upon graduation from Harvard University in Massachusetts at age twenty-one, he sold his portion of the family estate to study painting in London, England. He immediately enrolled at the Royal Academy, where he studied under Benjamin West (1738–1820) and was also inspired by the works of romantic painter Henry Fuseli. At that time, his paintings showed his subjective interpretation of nature and his fondness for the marvelous and mysterious.

After two years, he left to travel throughout Europe, visiting Italy, where he met the English romantic poet Samuel T. Coleridge (1772–1834). While in Italy, he acquired the title of "the American Titian," in reference to the Italian painter Titian (1487?–1576), famous for his color schemes.

Allston broke from the prevalent thought in the United States that color and light were minor elements in painting. His landscapes emphasized ambiguous shapes, and he used texture and color to express feeling. Allston was also famous for his under-painting to give more light to his works.

Always torn between his conflicting feelings for the United States and Europe, he travelled continuously between the two. On one trip to Europe in 1811, he took one of his art students, Samuel F. B. Morse (1791–1872), who later invented the telegraph and Morse code.

Allston's first work of importance was *The Dead Man Restored to Life by Touching the Bones of Elijah* (1813), which combined the classical form and romanticism.

Allston was also at the center of American

Washington Allston

intellectualism through his writings and lectures. His essays titled *Lectures in Art* revealed his classical viewpoints and were published after his death. He also wrote poetry, making typical analogies between the moods of nature and the moods of man. In 1813, his book of poems *The Sylphs of the Seasons and Other Poems* was published.

Four years later, he began painting *Belshazzar's Feast,* which remained unfinished, but attempted to combine his ideas of logic and classical views with romanticism. He also began to paint in a simpler, dreamlike fashion and often used women in dim landscapes as his subject. The delicate tones of his painting are most evident in *Moonlit Landscape* (1819).

Samuel T. Coleridge wrote to him once, saying, "To you alone of all contemporary painters does it seem to have been given to know what nature is."

John James Audubon

Born on April 26, 1785, Jean Jacques Fougere Audubon was born out of wedlock to a chambermaid and the sea captain Jean Audubon, who was temporarily docked in Haiti, then known as Santo Domingo. His mother died soon after his birth, and his father brought him to France to live with his wife and other children. As a boy, Audubon began drawing pictures of birds on his own, without instruction. He was a temperamental child who did not do well in school, and his father sent him to the United States at age eighteen to save him from military service and make him a more responsible and serious person.

While in the United States, Audubon resided in an estate of his father's near Philadelphia, Pennsylvania. There, Audubon told his neighbors that he was the son of Louis XVI and Marie-Antoinette and had been taken out of France as a child to save him from death by the guillotine during the French Revolution.

He continued to draw birds, and in 1808, he married Lucy Bakewell, who later support-ed him financially while he travelled and painted. Two years later, he left for Kentucky to try his fortune as a merchant and a speculator in real estate.

He declared bankruptcy in 1819 and was imprisoned for his unpaid debts. After his release, he moved to Ohio and made a living teaching and doing crayon portraits.

At thirty-five years of age, he exhibited his bird drawings at the Western Museum in Cincinnati, Ohio, and was received with laudatory reviews. The reception he received convinced him that he should travel across the United States and paint birds in their natural habitats.

Without money or experience, Audubon established himself in New Orleans, Louisiana, and began to collect specimens, painting more than one thousand subjects. Trying to establish himself as an artist, he learned to wire the bodies of different kinds of birds into natural positions of flight, feeding, or battle, painting each bird in its exact size. He emphasized the beauty of the contours by using natural lines without distortions. To reproduce color and texture, he used a combination of watercolor, pastels, and tempera, a painting technique in which a mixture of water and egg yolk is used as a binding medium to add sheen to areas.

After meeting with disappointment in his first showing, where scientists questioned the natural science of his work, he sailed for England with a portfolio of 240 paintings. His work impressed the critics there; they called it "an expression of wild abundance in America." In 1838, he completed 435 life-sized engravings titled *The Birds of America*. From 1831 to 1839, he collaborated with William MacGillivray to write an accompaniment to the paintings. Entitled *Ornithological Biography*, it was a biographical account of his fascination with birds, describing their flight behavior, their habits, and their cries.

HONORÉ DAUMIER
(1808–1879)

A French caricaturist, painter, and sculptor and a notable political and social satirist, Honoré Daumier (doe-me-YAY) devoted his paintings to everyday themes and social protest. The son of a glazier, he was born on February 26, 1808, in Marseille, but he moved to Paris with his family as a boy.

As soon as Daumier was old enough to know his way around, he began to work as a messenger for the bailiff of the law courts. During that time, he began to draw and take lessons from a friend of his father's, Alexandre Lenoir. At nineteen, he was supporting himself as a lithographer, and he studied for a brief period of time at the Académie Suisse. He began his artistic career by making drawings for advertisements. He became a staff member of the comic journal *La Caricature* and made a reputation for himself as a bold, satirical artist, becoming the most feared political cartoonist in France. His manner of drawing was spontaneous and the contour of the figure gave subjects a sense of nervous energy.

One of his caricatures, published in 1832, depicted King Louis Philippe (1773–1850) as *Gargantua*, a gigantic creature from romance conjured by author Rabelais (1494–1553). The caricature showed the king gorging on baskets of gold taken from the poor, and Daumier was imprisoned for six months as a result. He was allowed to spend half his sentence in a sanatorium and the other half in prison. At the time he wrote, "I'm getting four times as much work done in my new boarding house as I did at papa's."

Upon his release, he again returned to satirizing bourgeois society in the journal *Le Charivari*. He also began to satirize political subjects during the Revolution of 1848 in France, enjoying enormous popularity with his series *Robert Macaire*. The law courts were satirized in the series *Parliamentary Idylls*, while the hardships of the poor were depicted in *The Representatives Represented*.

Deeply interested in people, his paintings were satirical portrayals of everyday life. He did not include decorative elements in his works, and the colors in his paintings were compared to those in Rembrandt's works (see no. 26). Daumier's style was labeled baroque, and he never made a commercial success of his painting. Daumier's most celebrated work is *The Third Class Carriage* (1862?), which depicts a group of travelers on a train. The painting was created simply, utilizing minimal lines, where the hands of passengers are reduced to mere outlines while the bodies are solid.

Upon Daumier's death on February 11, 1879, his coffin was layered with flowers as a substitute for traditional velvet cloth. The local church refused to drape the coffin of a man who professed a humanitarian love for his fellow peers over the love of the Christian God.

Honoré Daumier

English photographer Julia Margaret Cameron made a series of photographic portraits of the great men of her day, including the writers Charles Darwin (1809–1882), Alfred Lord Tennyson (1809–1892), Henry Wadsworth Longfellow (1807–1882), and Robert Browning (1812–1889). She also photographed the astronomer Sir John Frederick William Herschel (1792–1871).

She was born on June 11, 1815, in Calcutta, India. She was the third daughter of James Prattle, a high civil servant from England in the East India Company. James Prattle raised his daughter on strict Victorian principles. At the age of twenty-three, she married Charles Hay Cameron. Charles was then forty-three years old, and he was a member of the Supreme Council of India. The couple had six children and settled in London, England, in 1848.

She was almost fifty years old when she began to be a serious photographer. She was presented with a camera as a gift from her daughters in order to begin a hobby. She converted her garden greenhouse into a darkroom and studio and worked for ten years straight. Friends, family, servants, and even passersby were coerced into modeling for pictures.

Her photographs were notable for their extreme close-ups, suppression of detail, and dramatic lighting. Her technique for drawing out the expression of the person, rather than a mere reflection, was regarded to have been ahead of her time.

Although sometimes criticized for poor focus and pictures smeared with fingerprints, she said that she was "interested in spiritual depth, not technical perfection." Her photographs were influenced by the romantic Pre-Raphaelite paintings of the time. These paintings reflected the materialism of industrialized England and imitated the style of Italian painters prior to Raphael (see no. 13). Her friend and mentor, George Frederic Watts, also inspired her to create beauty. Among her works were *Annie, My First Success* (1864), *Sir Joshua Herschel* (1867), and *Mrs. Herbert Duckworth* (1867).

At the request of the writer Lord Tennyson, she illustrated his book, *Idylls of the King*, with her photographs. The book was published in 1874, as was her autobiography *Annals of my Glass House*.

Cameron's photographs were brought to the limelight when they were discovered by photographer and art dealer Alfred Stieglitz (see no. 64). Legend holds that she continued to photograph until her death on January 26, 1879, and her last word was "beautiful."

Julia Cameron

ROSA BONHEUR
(1822–1899)

Rosa Bonheur

Specializing in animal subjects, painter Marie Rosalie Bonheur (bon-URR), known as Rosa, was the first woman to receive the Cross of the French Legion of Honor. She was born on March 22, 1822, in Bordeaux, France, to artistic parents. Her mother, Sophie Marqui, was a student in the drawing class of Rosa's father, Raymond Bonheur.

The family moved to Paris when she was seven years old, and there she visited the art galleries where she copied the works of the great artists.

She quit school at age twelve when her mother died, and she helped to raise her siblings, spending her free time sketching animals in the fields. She often dressed like a boy in her teens to be able to roam about freely. She found the attire convenient and continued to dress like a man in her adult years.

By the time she was seventeen, she was earning money selling copies of paintings she completed at the Louvre and found the direction of her art with her portraits of animals.

Concerned about the anatomical correctness of her art, she obtained limbs of animals from butcher shops to dissect and study. She also visited horse fairs and cattle markets to observe and sketch from life. Rosa described her art and herself as "matter of fact in everything." Her work demonstrates a strong sense of movement and lyrical effects of light to lend a romantic feeling to her paintings.

As her fame grew, admirers throughout Europe sent her animal parts to draw. Her first appearance at the annual Paris exhibition in 1841, with the paintings *Goats and Sheep* and *Two Rabbits* was well received. In 1849, her picture *Plowing in Nivernais*, a pastoral scene taken directly from nature studies in the country, was purchased by the government for its permanent collection at the Luxembourg Gallery.

Her greatest reward came when she won the first-class medal for her picture *Horse Fair* (1853?). It is remarkable for its dynamic movement and the use of light to add energy to the painting and the ten life-size horses. In 1864, she received the Cross of the Legion of Honor from Empress Eugenie, who was acting as a representative for her husband, Napolean III.

Rosa's philosophy of art was the verse written by her favorite author, George Sand (1804–1876), "Art for art's sake is a vain word. Art for truth, art for the beautiful and the good, that is the religion I seek for." A technical perfectionist, Bonheur would often allow two years for drying the thick underpainting she applied to her pictures. She died on May 25, 1899.

Mathew Brady

Mathew Brady, best known for his photographs of politicians and the American Civil War (1861–1865), was a native of Warren County, New York. No records of his birth or childhood have been discovered, but around 1844, he opened his own business, Brady's Daguerrean Miniature Gallery, and set out to photograph the famous and wealthy in American society. He felt that he would be serving history by documenting its great figures in photographs. During Brady's fifty years as a photographer, he photographed the U.S. Presidents, from John Quincy Adams to William McKinley, the sixth through the twenty-fifth presidents. (The only exception was President William Henry Harrison, who died a month after his inauguration, so Brady never got a chance to photograph him.)

He perfected the daguerreotype method of photography, in which a direct positive image on a silver plate, exposed to sunlight, could record a sharp image in half an hour. He was notable for inventing a number of the tricks of successful photography, probably through trial and error, such as rubbing a freckled face until it was bright red, because without a uniform appearance, any spots could appear blotchy. He also raised or lowered the camera to correct a distorted face or long neck, insisted that gloves be worn by women with long fingers, and so on.

At the outbreak of the American Civil War, Brady invested $100,000 to record the event in photographs. Brady assumed the government would buy his photographs after the war ended. He hired men to cover the territory and take pictures. Brady paid the photographers $35 a week, taking the credit for the actual shot. He was intent on making the only complete pictorial history of the Civil War. He began to ignore his accumulating bills for photography chemicals and glass plates. Brady personally photographed some battles, such as the Battle of Bull Run (1861), the Battle of Antietam (1862), and the Battle of Gettysburg (1863).

A Brady Civil War photograph was posed and grandiose. Brady would take charge of a scene, asking a general to stand in a favorable position for the camera, or telling a wounded man to remain still, or ordering gun batteries into different positions to improve the composition. He created a technique of presenting the war in dramatic appeal.

The government showed no interest in his photographs, and Brady declared bankruptcy in 1873. The War Department later purchased his photographs at a public auction for $2,840. Brady died on January 15, 1896, from a kidney problem, alone, poor and forgotten at Presbyterian Hospital, New York.

GUSTAVE MOREAU
(1826–1898)

A French symbolist painter who emphasized the morbid side of life and death, Gustave Moreau exemplified the term "decadent." Born on April 6, 1826, in Paris, Moreau, the son of an architect, enrolled at the government-sponsored art school Ecole des Beaux-Arts, at the age of twenty. He was first taught by the neoclassical painter Francois-Edouard Picot, but Moreau's mature style was not formed until 1850, when he came in contact with Theodore Chassériau.

Moreau was dominated by the desire to represent the legendary and divine in art. He painted literary and mythological subjects in an imaginative way, using rich colors, which he heightened in tone by using wax when mixing the colors.

His landscapes were often depicted with steep and rocky cliffs and twisted trees, set against light distant backgrounds. He found inspiration in the Koran, the bible of Muslim prophecy, as well as Egyptian, Greek, and Oriental mythology. He often combined details from each book to depict universal concerns in fairy tale form.

His famous pieces that demonstrate the dark hues and subject matter include *Oedipus and the Sphinx* (1864) and *The Young and Death* (1865). After receiving hostile criticism, he withdrew from exhibiting at the official Salon from 1869 to 1876, and in 1880, he stopped exhibiting altogether and closed himself off from society.

In 1892, after years of solitary life, he became a professor at the Ecole des Beaux-Arts. He was a teacher who cultivated the individual talents of his students, among them Henri Matisse (see no. 68) and Georges Rouault (see no. 69).

Moreau's vision appealed to symbolist writers, such as the novelist J. K. Huysmans, who pursued similar feelings in their works. He also held a strong attraction to the surrealist artists whose works emphasized dream imagery and the unconscious.

In 1898, Moreau left his estate and eight thousand paintings to France to create a museum. His former student, Rouault, became the first curator of the collection.

Gustave Moreau

Romantic religious painter Dante Gabriel Rossetti was born in London, England, on May 12, 1828. His father, the Italian poet Gabriel Rossetti, was living in exile from Italy for his liberal views. Rossetti's artistic education began at age nine, with drawing lessons at King's College, which he attended until age fifteen. He then took private lessons from the painter Ford Madox Brown (1821–1893) and also enrolled at the Royal Academy, where he was described as rambunctious with an impertinent tongue and a flamboyant appearance.

At the academy, Rossetti met the painters Sir John Everett Millais and Holman Hunt and with them founded the Pre-Raphaelite Brotherhood. This movement imitated the style of Italian painters prior to Raphael (see no. 13). The movement also was preoccupied with the medieval past and a rejection of materialism of the industrialized world. The past was conceived to be a time of harmonious union between the individual and society. For Rossetti, the ambiance of the Middle Ages allowed chivalry and love to flourish. His subjects were influenced by the writings of Dante Alighieri, author of *The Divine Comedy*.

Love was the main theme in Rossetti's paintings. He painted only one type of woman, known as the Rossetti girl. Her face was sad and vacant, suggesting sensuality. She had a long neck, a flowing weight of hair, and dark protruding eyes. The only distinguishable feature among each of the women was the color of her hair.

The woman he most immortalized in his paintings was Elizabeth Eleanor Siddal, whom he married in 1860. The most notable of these works were *Mary Magdalene at the House of Simon the Pharisee* (1858?) and *Beata Beatrix* (1863). Other renowned paintings include *Monna Vanna* (1866) and *Prosperine* (1874). Elizabeth committed suicide in 1862 after contracting tuberculosis and giving birth to a stillborn son.

Rossetti was also renowned as a poet. At Elizabeth's funeral, he placed the only copy of his unpublished poems in her coffin. In 1869, however, he had the coffin raised to retrieve his work.

When he was in his mid-thirties, he alienated himself from society. At this time, he was living in an apartment with a private collection of birds and a kangaroo, among other animals. In 1872, he collapsed due to an addiction to chloral hydrate, which he used as a sleeping pill. He recovered temporarily and continued to paint and write poetry, but he maintained his addiction. In 1881, at the age of fifty-three, he had an attack of paralysis and died on April 9, 1882.

Dante Rossetti

CAMILLE PISSARRO
(1830–1903)

A French impressionist painter of landscapes and river scenes, Camille Jacob Pissarro lived by his own motto: "One must have only one master—nature." Born in St. Thomas, Virgin Islands, he showed an early interest in drawing and painting, despite his father's belief that art was not serious learning. Pissarro worked at his father's store until he was twelve years old, then left for France to complete his education. Homesick and unable to concentrate on his studies, he covered his books with drawings of banana trees, plantations, and other memories of the tropics. When Pissarro was seventeen, he returned to the island upon his father's demand that he assist with the family business. At twenty-two, he ran away to Venezuela with a fellow painter, Fritz Melbye, whom he met sketching on the docks. Three years later, he returned to Paris to pursue the study of art.

Camille Pissarro

He first attended the government-supported art school Ecole des Beaux-Arts and then studied at the Académie Suisse. It was at the Académie that he first met the impressionist painter Claude Monet (see no. 50), in 1859. That same year, he had a picture accepted into the Salon, the nationally supported art gallery. Pissarro had approached the painter Jean-Baptiste-Camille Corot (1796–1875), whom he idolized, and obtained his permission to name him as his teacher in his submission to the Salon. Although Pissarro exhibited at intervals in the Salon, he was rejected by Corot, who found his technique too "free." His style incorporated a spontaneous quality with a light brush stroke that viewed nature in a sympathetic manner.

In 1874, Pissarro exhibited in the first impressionist show and was the only artist to exhibit in all eight succeeding impressionist exhibits. As the oldest member of the group, he served as a mentor to Paul Cezanne, Mary Cassatt, and Paul Gauguin (see nos. 48, 54 and 55).

At fifty-six years of age, Pissarro, even though he himself was considered an impressionist painter, joined a revolt with the pointillist artists, who were against the brush stroke of the impressionist painters. Pointillist artists instead used dabs of pure color to produce intense color effects. After ten years, Pissarro realized that pointillism was too restrictive for him, and he returned to impressionism. At this time, he finally achieved some recognition for his work. The painting *Bather in Woods* (1895) demonstrates his use of light to invoke feeling.

Failing health at age sixty-five forced him to paint indoors. From windows, he painted Paris cityscapes. Figures and carriages moved through the street, displaying life and energy; trees against the buildings were depicted in large scale; and the skies were filled with light and clouds. Pissarro's genius was his ability to portray life and order, movement and stability, and change within constancy in nature. In 1898, Pissarro painted his series of the *Avenue de l'Opera*, which consisted of eight views of the street from the Theatre Français.

He refused to label his style of work, but others think of Edouard Manet (mah-NAY) as the forerunner of French Impressionism. He was born in Paris on January 23, 1832, to a high government official, and Manet was expected to follow his father in a legal career. After finishing his studies at Collège Rollin, in 1848, he went to sea as an apprentice cadet to avoid going into the legal profession.

In 1850, when he failed the entrance exam to the navy, Manet's father allowed him to pursue an art career at the studio of Thomas Couture. He studied with Couture for six years, then travelled throughout Europe, visiting the galleries and museums to copy the works of the masters.

His portrayal of everyday subject matter would prove to be influential to French painting and the development of modern art. Manet used bold brush strokes when he painted, in order to accentuate realism in his subject matters. His subject matters included common people, including beggars, street urchins, and cafe characters. Typically, his figures maintain an alert glance and stare directly at the viewer, always giving the feeling that both the artist and the subject are observing one another. Manet used the technique known as peinture claire, whereby the subject of the painting is lighted from the front, illuminating shadows.

His most famous painting, *Le dejeuner sur l'herbe* (1863), portrays a picnic scene, where a nude female is attended to by two fully dressed young men. The work was attacked by critics as indecent, which in turn made Manet a leader in the dispute between the academic and the rebellious art factions of his time. The painting *Olympia* (1865?) also made him the focus of controversy. This portrait of a nude female in a modern setting was accepted into the official Salon, but it met with bad reviews. Manet's idea of success was measured by his acceptance into the government-sponsored Salon, even though he rejected the principles for which it stood.

Manet was a pivotal figure in the controversy on the judgment of art that finally discredited the French Academy, the official judges. He created an uproar in a country whose artists were closely tied to government, by participating in the Salon des Refusés. The works rejected by the Salon were to be displayed, and the public was given the opportunity to decide whether the jury had been right or wrong in rejecting the paintings.

Throughout his career, Manet was a painter of contemporary life. A year before his death, he was nominated for the Legion of Honor for his contributions to the technical style of nineteenth-century art. He died in Paris on April 30, 1883.

Edouard Manet

James Abbott McNeill Whistler embodied the image of the cosmopolitan artist. He was born on July 11, 1834, in Lowell, Massachusetts. His father was a distinguished military engineer. At age nine, his family moved to St. Petersburg, Russia, where he attended the Imperial Academy. His father died when Whistler was fifteen years old, at which point he returned to the United States. Two years later, he was admitted to the U.S. Military Academy at West Point. His own tastes were not military, however, and his studies suffered. He was dismissed from the academy three years later. He then made an unsuccessful attempt to enter the navy and finally obtained a position as a draftsman in the Coast Survey Department in Washington, D.C., which was established to map the United States coastlines for military purposes. It was there that he learned etching. The tediousness of the work soon tired him, and in 1855, he left for Paris, where he studied painting under Charles Gabriel Gleyre.

Through Gleyre, Whistler obtained unlimited access to the Louvre museum and the privilege to set up an easel and copy the artwork. Whistler was talented in his combination of techniques acquired from past masters. He learned how to silhouette a figure against a bland background to create a full-length portrait and was noted for his avoidance of brilliant color and absence of detail. From Japanese prints, he acquired the skill of creating shapes, and from Oriental ceramics, he borrowed the flowing decorative techniques. His work emphasized a relationship between color and music, and he used musical terms, such as nocturnes, harmonies, and symphonies, to describe his paintings.

Whistler loved scandal, welcoming it as a way of gaining fame. In 1863, his painting *White Girl* achieved notoriety at the Salon des Refusés. In 1875, he exhibited *Nocturnes in*

James McNeill Whistler

Black and Gold: Falling Rocket, in which globs of paint represent embers floating down through a dark sky. The painting shocked audiences with its revolutionary style, and critic John Ruskin accused Whistler of "flinging a pot of paint in the public's face." Whistler sued Ruskin and won.

Moving to England, Whistler was regarded as arrogant, witty, satirical, and an expert in *The Gentle Art of Making Enemies*, the title of the only book he wrote. The book consisted of recordings of his quarrels with art associations and was published in 1890.

He also devoted much time to lithography, which he brought to perfection. As an etcher, he was second only to Rembrandt (see no. 26). He completed roughly 150 lithographs and over 400 etchings, which he exhibited at the Fine Arts Society in London. In 1886, he was elected president of the Society of British Artists. When he and his friends left the society in 1888, Whistler remarked that "the artists had come out and the British had remained."

Hilaire Germain Edgar Degas (deh-GAH) was the oldest of five children. He was born into a wealthy family in the banking business in Paris, France, on July 19, 1834. He visited the Louvre museum often while he studied law. When he was twenty years old, he decided to become a painter. He enrolled at the Ecole des Beaux-Arts, the government-sponsored art school, but two years later, he left for Italy to study the masters.

While in Rome, he visited relatives and completed the portrait *The Bellelli Family* (1859), which is noted for its acute perception of four personalities. His paintings were characterized by movement and continuity of lines. He returned to Paris in 1861 and was commissioned to complete a series of paintings for the government-sponsored Salon. In 1870, with the outbreak of the Franco-Prussian War, Degas enlisted in the artillery. While recuperating from the experience, he decided never to exhibit at the Salon again.

After a trip to New Orleans, Louisiana, in 1872, where he first became aware of losing his eyesight, he returned to Paris where he discovered a new subject—the female form and the ballet. Known as the "painter of dancers," Degas sketched from live models in his studio, where he could control the factors of form and composition. He combined different poses into groups that depicted dancers on stage, either stretching or performing.

In 1873, Degas was among the founding members of the impressionist group, who are known for their direct observation of nature. Other impressionist painters include Camille Pissarro, Claude Monet, and Auguste Renoir, (see nos. 44, 50, and 52).

Failing eyesight led Degas to devote more of his attention to sculpture. Through sculpture, as in his painting, he captured the action of movement; his female figures, notably ballet dancers, are depicted in poses that demonstrate the physical exertion of dance.

Believing that a painter could have no personal life, he never married, explaining that "there is love and there is work, and we have but a single heart." Degas spent the last twenty years of his life in seclusion and died on September 27, 1917, in Paris.

Edgar Degas

During the greater part of his lifetime, Paul Cezanne (say-ZAHN), who initiated the revolution in modern art by shifting the emphasis from realism to abstraction, was largely ignored and worked in isolation.

Cezanne was born in the town of Aix-en-Provence in southern France, on January 19, 1839. His father, Louis-Auguste Cezanne, was a wealthy banker who disapproved of Cezanne's early artistic interests, but allowed him to study drawing at the Aix museum. At the same time, Cezanne received a classical education at the College Bourbon. He did not have any companions until age thirteen, when he met Emile Zola (1840–1902), who was to become a prominent author. The two remained friends until 1886, when Cezanne became bitter over what he assumed to be a reference to his failures in one of Zola's novels and estranged himself from his oldest friend and supporter.

Paul Cezanne

At age twenty-three, after a number of bitter family disputes, Cezanne was given a small allowance and sent to study art in Paris. He never had any formal training but worked by copying the models at the Académie Suisse. Cezanne represented contemporary life. He painted the world he observed rather than painting an idealized version of his still lifes, landscapes, and portraits. The most significant influence on his work was Camille Pissarro (see no. 44), who gave Cezanne the encouragement he needed. Pissarro also introduced Cezanne to new impressionist techniques and encouraged him to lighten his colors and break away from his brooding moods.

In 1869, Cezanne met the model Hortense Fiquet, whom he formed a relationship with and later married. Afraid that his father would disinherit him for his choice in a bride, he kept her existence from him for years.

Cezanne had a way of imparting density to the structure of individual objects; covering the entire canvas, he conveyed the illusion of space by overlapping planes and painting in patches of color. Although he painted from nature, he would distort shapes or change colors of objects to give more depth to the work. Always regarded as an eccentric, Cezanne never sold a painting in his lifetime. His most famous work was *House of the Hanged Man, Auvers* (1874). Other works that express forms in space were *The Kitchen Table* (1890) and *The Card Players* (1892).

On October 15, 1906, he was painting in the fields and was caught in a storm. He died a week later.

Sculptor Francois Auguste René Rodin (roe-DAN) is distinguished for his realism as well as for conveying both the positive and negative aspects of humanity, such as beauty and anxiety, in his work.

The son of a police official, Rodin was born in Paris, France, on November 12, 1840. He began studying art at age fourteen by attending the Petite Ecole, a school of decorative arts, and visiting the Louvre museum. On three occasions, he attempted and failed to gain admittance to the Ecole des Beaux-Arts.

At eighteen, in order to earn a living, he began to work for other sculptors, including Ernest Carrier-Belleuse. When he was twenty-two, the death of his sister Maria traumatized him so greatly that he joined an order of monks.

Auguste Rodin

Leaving the monastery when he was twenty-four years old, he met the seamstress Rose Beuret, who became his life companion and a model for many of his works. That same year, he submitted his work *Man with a Broken Nose* (1864) to the government-sponsored Salon; it was rejected initially and later accepted under the title *Portrait of a Roman*. The success inspired him to travel to Italy, where he was influenced by the work of Michelangelo (see no. 11). He came back to Paris and created his *Age of Bronze* (1877). The work depicted a male nude figure and showed extreme realism. It created a controversy and caused accusations that Rodin had made plaster casts from living models. The episode brought him more fame than harm.

Rodin had the ability to convey feeling through facial expression and individual parts of the body. He cut the hollows of the face deeply to create strong shadows, while his textured surface heightened the sense of life and movement, a technique not seen in the impersonal smoothness of classical sculpture.

Rodin considered beauty to be a truthful representation of inner states. Thus, he did not distort the anatomy of his sculptures.

In 1880, he was commissioned by the French government to design a pair of doors for a museum of decorative arts that was to be built. The project, known as *The Gates of Hell*, absorbed Rodin for the remainder of his life, although it was still unfinished at his death. He collaborated on the project with Camille Claudel (see no. 63) with whom he had a relationship. Rodin always worked in grand scale, and most of his works depicted human suffering, such as *The Thinker* (1888) and *The Prodigal Son* (1885).

At seventy-six years old, Rodin donated his works to the French government. Still placed as Rodin set them, they are in the Musee Rodin at the Hotel Biron in Paris.

50. CLAUDE MONET
(1840–1926)

The French impressionist painter Claude Monet (moe-NAY) was born in Paris on November 14, 1840, but spent most of his childhood in Le Havre, where his father owned a grocery store. At fifteen, he was selling his own drawings on the street, and four years later, he had committed himself to a career as a painter and moved to Paris to study at the Académie Suisse. Forced to complete military service soon after, he returned to Paris in 1862 and studied under Charles Gleyre. While at Gleyre's studio, he befriended Edouard Manet (see no. 45) and Auguste Renoir (see no. 52).

Monet was noted for extreme detail, using loose brush strokes, bold colors, and the changing effect of light in his studies of nature. His first success was the acceptance of the portrait of his mistress Camille, *The Green Dress* (1866), in the official Salon. After that, he was continually rejected. He became too poor to buy painting supplies and resorted to soliciting his friends for money.

Monet and his friends, Camille Pissarro, Edgar Degas, Paul Cezanne (see nos. 44, 47, and 48), and others, formed their own exhibition in 1874 that they hoped would have more prestige than the Salon des Refusés.

Impressionism is characterized by a direct observation of nature. The word impressionism is derived from the title of Monet's painting *Impression, Sunrise* (1873). A critic said the painting reminded him of wallpaper because the work appeared sketchy and unfinished.

In 1880, a year after his wife's death, his painting was accepted into the Salon. Monet was not pleased with the position the painting was given and refused to exhibit there again.

Six years later, he began to gain recognition and painted the two series *Haystacks* and *Poplars,* which depict a single scene painted numerous times with variations of light, shadow, and season.

At the age of fifty-two, Monet remarried

Claude Monet

to Alice Hoschede. Together, they settled in Giverny, France. It was in Giverny that he began painting the series *Water Lilies* (1900–1926). These large canvases show a rhythm of the brush stroke, appearing abstract in pattern, which could stand on its own without the focus of the subject, but is combined with visions of water, light, and foliage to translate a simple pond into a visual spectacle of paint.

Berthe Morisot

Berthe Morisot's (MOR-e-so) career and success as an impressionist painter, characterized by a direct observation of nature, were remarkable in that she was one of the first women to challenge the established art circles. She was the youngest of three daughters of an upper-middle-class family, born in Bourges, France, on January 14, 1841. Her father had studied at the Ecole des Beaux-Arts before becoming a government official.

Morisot began to draw as a child, taking lessons seriously at age seventeen with Joseph-Benoit Guichard, whom she persuaded to allow her to paint outdoors. Two years later, she was introduced to the painter Jean-Baptiste-Camille Corot (1796–1875), who became her teacher. Her early style was characterized by subtle color harmonies.

At twenty-three, she debuted at the official Salon with two landscapes and was accepted regularly to exhibit for the next ten years.

At twenty-seven, she was introduced to Edouard Manet (see no. 45), who became her mentor, a major influence on her work, and her brother in-law. Morisot also posed for many of Manet's paintings. Under Manet's guidance, Morisot's brush stroke became fast and loose, using broad strokes to depict planes. Details were eliminated from her paintings, and her colors were bolder. She focused on representing the changing effects of light. Her work conveyed a sense of spontaneity, as in *The Sisters* (1869), which shows two figures seated in a parlor, representative of a common scene in everyday life. She often painted women in outdoor or domestic settings. In 1873, she exhibited her painting *The Cradle*, and her former teacher, Guichard, wrote a letter to her mother saying that the work was that of a "madman."

When she was thirty-three, she abandoned showing at the Salon, choosing to exhibit with the impressionists. That same year she married Eugène Manet.

In 1892, her first one-woman show was held at the Boussad and Valadon Gallery. Two years later, the French government bought her work *Young Woman Dressing for a Ball* (1884?). The freshness of her style and the intimacy she captured in her work made her a significant artist in the rebellion against the factions that dominated the art world at the time.

Unlike other impressionist painters, Pierre-Auguste Renoir (ren-WAHR) was interested in painting the single human figure or family groups more than landscapes. Born to a tailor on February 25, 1841, in Limoges, France, Renoir began an artistic career as a child. He painted designs on china in a Paris porcelain factory. At seventeen, he copied paintings from pictures at the Louvre museum onto fans, lampshades, and blinds. By the time he was twenty-one, he had begun to study painting formally at the academy of Charles Gleyre in Paris. There he met Claude Monet, Camille Pissarro and Paul Cezanne (see nos. 50, 44, and 48). Together they formed the impressionist group.

Noted for his radiant and intimate paintings, usually portraying sensual figures of women, he used harmony of lines and brilliant color to express mood. In 1874, Renoir led the first impressionist exhibition. He had a personal exhibition five years later, organized by the publisher Georges Charpentier, for whom Renoir painted family portraits.

After the first impressionist show, Renoir was torn between maintaining the theme of painting outdoors and his true passion to paint in the studio. Renoir's masterpieces of the time demonstrate his conflict of interest.

The painting *The Swing* (1876) was painted in his garden and depicts a young girl on a rope swing while an admirer stands idly by. The painting was said to lack the spontaneous vision he captured in his famous *Moulin de la Galette* (1876), painted in the studio. That work showed a group of dancers, carefully organized to appear as if the group were captured at a fleeting moment.

Other works of this period were *Madame Charpentier and Her Children* (1878), *Two Little Circus Girls* (1879), and *The Luncheon of the Boating Party* (1881).

At forty, he travelled to Algeria and Italy, where he was influenced by the works of Raphael (see no. 13) and began a more classical style of painting. He painted in strictly defined forms, as evident in *Bathers* (1887).

Nine years after his travels, he married Aline Charigot and had three sons, whom he painted in many works.

During the last twenty years of his life, Renoir was crippled by arthritis and unable to move his hands freely. He continued to paint by adapting his style to looser brush strokes and painting with the brush strapped to his arm.

Auguste Renoir

Henri Rousseau

Henri Rousseau (roo-SO), known as *Le Douanier* in reference to his former position as a minor inspector with the Paris Customs Office, was the most celebrated of "naive" artists, a term used to classify untrained painters. The son of a dealer in tinware, born on May 21, 1844, Rousseau served in the army for four years prior to obtaining a post at the customs office in 1871. He claimed that he had visited Mexico while in the army, which he said influenced the subject of his paintings, but no proof exists to substantiate this. Rousseau did not begin to paint until he was almost forty years old and was completely self-taught. When he was forty-nine, he accepted early retirement so that he could devote himself entirely to painting. To supplement his small pension, he gave drawing and music lessons.

Rousseau's imaginative paintings were characterized by fantastical subjects and disproportions of the figures. A lack of training in anatomy and perspective gave his paintings a sense of innocence.

He is best known for his jungle scenes, most notably *Surprised! Tropical Storm with a Tiger* (1891) and *Sleeping Gypsy* (1897). These imaginative paintings were exotic, detailed perceptions of animal and plant life, which were derived from his visits to the zoos and botanical gardens of Paris. The last of these works, *The Dream* (1910), culminates the magical quality of his scenery.

Rousseau exhibited regularly at art shows organized by experimental artists. Although he was often ridiculed by critics and the public, he interpreted their sarcastic remarks as praise. His work showed an irrational configuration of object and form, which was adopted by surrealist artists.

In 1908, his work was discovered by Pablo Picasso (see no. 71). Picasso bought Rousseau's paintings and attended many of his gatherings. Recognition of Rousseau's art opened the way for other untrained artists to to gain acknowledgement.

Rousseau died on September 2, 1910, in Paris, France.

In spite of the fact that she was an American, Mary Cassatt was welcomed into the group of European impressionist painters, who emphasized light and color in their depictions of nature. The fifth of seven children of Robert and Katherine Cassatt, born in Allegheny City, Pennsylvania, on May 22, 1844, Cassatt was a descendant of a wealthy family and had the opportunity to travel to Europe as a young child. Inspired by artists' exhibitions in Paris as a young girl, she was determined to become a painter. She began studying at the Pennsylvania Academy of Fine Arts at age seventeen, then in Paris at age twenty-one under the tutelage of Charles Joshua Chopin.

Her work was accepted in the Salon, the government-sponsored museum in France, before she joined the impressionist movement, or "independents" as she preferred to call them, upon the invitation of Edgar Degas (see no. 47). The impressionists were in defiance of the jury system that selected paintings to be displayed in the Salon. They also wanted to elevate their status above the admittance to the Salon des Refusés, which did not discriminate against any artists. Cassatt exhibited with the impressionists in 1879, 1880, 1881, and 1886. She developed a lifelong friendship with Degas, who also painted her portrait.

Cassatt's paintings focus on the objective reality of the subject, mostly women or children involved in everyday activities. Capturing reality through patterns of light and color, she was influenced by Degas in her precise drawing and casual arrangement of her subjects. She began to emphasize line after viewing an exhibition of Japanese prints in 1890. This is evident in the *Bath* (1892). Other important works include *The Boating Party* (1892?), *The Letter* (1893?), and *Mother Feeding her Child* (1893?).

She was instrumental in introducing impressionism to the United States and in persuading American collectors to invest in the work of her colleagues in the group. In 1904, she was awarded the Legion of Honor, a medal confirming her success as an artist, which was notable in a time when the profession was dominated by men. She suffered from the deterioration of her eyesight in later years and was forced to stop painting in 1914. She died twelve years later of tuberculosis in Paris, where she spent most of her life and where she was first inspired to paint.

Mary Cassatt

The French post-impressionist painter Eugene Henri Paul Gauguin (go-GAN) was born in Paris on June 7, 1848, but moved to Lima, Peru, when he was three years old. Gauguin lived there until he was seven and was greatly influenced by the open, carefree culture of South America.

He returned to Paris to begin his education, and at seventeen, he joined the merchant marines as a navigation cadet, working his way into the navy at age twenty. When he was twenty-three, he returned to Paris to begin a career as a stockbroker, and two years later, he married Mette Sophie Gad.

He took up painting as a hobby, beginning classes at the Academie Colarossi. Developing an interest in impressionist art, he became an avid art collector and made acquaintance with Camille Pissarro (see no. 44) and Paul Signac (see no. 60). His first success came in 1876, when the painting *Landscape at Viroflay* (1875?) was accepted at the Salon, the government-sponsored art gallery. It was impressive for a first attempt.

In 1883, Gauguin abandoned his job as a stockbroker to devote himself to painting. Due to a lack of income, he was forced to move to Denmark to live with his in-laws. Leaving his wife in Denmark, he returned to Paris in 1885. Two years later, he travelled to Martinique in the West Indies where he became enamored with the exotic tropical country. The trip was influential in moving Gauguin's style away from impressionism and towards bright color and primitive art. He painted *Jacob Wrestling with the Angel* (1888) using his new style, termed synthetism. Synthetism is characterized by large, simplified forms, abstract shapes, and brilliant colors.

Continuing to travel, he settled in Tahiti from 1891 to 1893 and created the painting *Aha Oe Feii* (1892). On another stay in Tahiti, from 1895 to 1901, he painted *Holiday* (1896) and *Two Tahitian Women* (1899), which demonstrates his flat planes and abstract drawing of figures.

He longed for freedom from European constraints in artwork, and his work characterized that. His health began to deteriorate, and he died on May 8, 1903, on the Marquesas.

Paul Gauguin

Vincent van Gogh (van-GO), a Dutch post-impressionist painter, represents the epitome of emotional spontaneity in painting. The oldest of six children, born to a Protestant minister in Groot Zundert, Holland, on March 30, 1853, he was characterized as a moody, restless, and temperamental person throughout his life. He was also articulate and well read, with a wealth of knowledge that he displayed in his more than seven hundred letters to his brother Theo. The letters were published in 1911 and constitute a record of van Gogh's life.

At sixteen, van Gogh was sent to The Hague, Holland, to work for his uncle, a partner in an international firm of art dealers. There he studied painting with Anton Mauve. Failing to appeal to the clients, he was transferred to the London branch, then sent from uncle to uncle, until he alienated everyone with his preaching on the vulgarity and excesses of the rich. He enrolled in evangelical training in Belgium, which he soon abandoned to work as a lay preacher among the coal miners there. At the age of twenty-seven, he found his true calling—to be an artist.

Moving back to Holland, he painted his most famous piece of the period, which kept with his humanitarian views. *The Potato Eaters* (1885), dark and somber, expressed the misery and poverty of the people. Van Gogh wrote about the work, "I have tried to emphasize that those people, eating their potatoes in the lamplight, have dug the earth with those very hands they put in the dish."

That same year, he relocated to Antwerp, Belgium, where he enrolled at the Academy of Art. He entered the drawing class wearing his signature round fur cap, which would become famous in many self-portraits. The teacher felt van Gogh's strokes to be "too heavy," and van Gogh left the academy the second day. While in Antwerp, he was influenced by the works of Peter Paul Rubens (see no. 22) and by Japanese

Vincent van Gogh

print makers such as Hokusai (1760–1849).

Relocating to Paris in 1886, he abandoned the bold brush stroke and moralistic realism. He adopted brilliant colors to express symbolism in his scenes of fields, trees, and rustic life, such as *Night Watch (1888)* and *Starry Night (1889)*, which he painted in the countryside of Arles, France. He had gone to Arles to rest and invited the painter Paul Gauguin (see no. 55) to join him. It is rumored that the two painters argued vehemently, and one evening, van Gogh threatened Gauguin with a razor. The same night, feeling remorse for his actions, van Gogh cut off his own ear. The event was commemorated by van Gogh in *Self Portrait with Bandaged Ear* (1889). Van Gogh went to an asylum at St. Remy, France, producing 150 paintings in one year. His depression became more acute, and he shot himself on July 27, 1890, dying two days later. Van Gogh sold only one painting in his lifetime, *Red Vineyard at Arles* (1889).

57. GEORGES SEURAT
(1859–1891)

Georges Seurat (soo-RAH) originated the scientific technique of pointillism, also known as divisionism, one of the techniques in the French school of neo-impressionism. In pointillism, solid forms are built up through the application of many small dots of contrasting color on a white background.

Combining science and art, Seurat spent his life studying color theories and the effects of different line structures. He was born on December 2, 1859, in Paris. His father, Chrysostome Antoiñe Seurat, was a legal official, and his mother came from a family of jewelers.

Seurat began drawing as a child, and, at age fifteen, he left regular school to enroll at the local municipal drawing institute. The training prepared him to enter the Ecole des Beaux-Arts four years later, where he received a rigorous and standardized art training. At that time he was influenced by Rembrandt (see no. 26) and Francisco de Goya (see no. 33).

Seurat was interested in discovering an "optical formula" for art. He always drew from life and stressed the importance of a painting's ability to transmit moral views. In 1879, he left the Beaux-Arts for mandatory enlistment in the military. He maintained his artistic interests by drawing in a notebook. His military experience forced him to look for his subject matter in the world around him and further influenced his style of creating large compositions with small dots of color. This is most evident in his painting *Man Leaning on a Parapet* (1881).

He was first accepted to exhibit at the Salon in 1883 with the drawing *Aman-Jean* (1882?), but the next year his painting *Bathing at Asnières* (1882?) was refused.

Seurat and several other artists, including Paul Signac (see no. 60) then founded the Société des Artistes Indépendants in 1884. The exhibit allowed artists of all calibers to show their work regularly without the scrutiny of the jury system. The first show was chaotic, but it led to the establishment of a permanent residence for art outside the Salon. Thereafter, Seurat never submitted work to the Salon.

Seurat's subjects all revolve around a central figure acting out a role in society, since he felt felt that people in Paris were posing or performing at living. He is famous for his meticulous attention to detail, and his high reputation among artists was cemented with his paintings *The Bathers* (1884), a scene of boys bathing in the river, and the world-famous *A Sunday Afternoon on the Island of La Grande Jatte* (1886), representing Sunday strollers.

Georges Seurat

Without formal art training and largely self-educated, American painter Anna Mary Robertson Moses, better known as Grandma Moses, spent most of her life as a farmer's wife in Washington County, New York. She dropped out of school at age twelve to work on neighboring farms. At seventeen, she married Thomas Moses, and together they moved to Virginia. The couple returned to New York in 1905, and Moses painted her first picture in 1918, on the fireplace in her parlor. Two years later, she painted a picture on the panels of her pull-out table, which was later to become her easel.

Upon her husband's death in 1927, Grandma Moses moved to Vermont, where she stayed until 1935, when she again settled in New York. In her seventies, she began to substitute painting for embroidery, as it was less painful to her arthritic condition. Her first paintings were copies of postcards she received. Then in 1938, she began composing original works. A group of her paintings shown in a drugstore window was noticed by the art collector Louis Caldor, who succeeded in showing three of her paintings in the show Contemporary Unknown American Painters at the Museum of Modern Art, in New York City, in 1939.

Caldor brought her work to the attention of the art dealer Otto Kallir. Kallir gave Grandma Moses her first solo exhibition at the Galerie St. Etienne in 1940, titled What A Farm Wife Painted. That same year she was awarded the New York State Prize at the Syracuse Museum of Fine Arts for her work *The Old Oats Bucket* (1939?). Her uniqueness and primitive realistic views of life created a relationship between the

Grandma Moses

landscape and the subjects she focused on, such as a bridge or an automobile. She preferred to paint from memory.

Her work, such as *Thanksgiving Turkey* (circa 1943), *Sugaring Off* (1945), and *Out for the Christmas Tree* (1945), began to be reproduced in postcards, books, and greeting cards around the nation. In 1949, President Harry S. Truman presented her with the Women's National Press Club Award for outstanding accomplishments in art. She was also presented with two honorary doctorates, from Russell Sage College and Moore Institute of Art. It was not until she was ninety years old that her work toured Europe, gaining her an international reputation.

As a painter, Grandma Moses was a realist who depicted life as she lived and saw it. Her pictures always maintained a positive outlook. She once stated that she would not paint anything she knew nothing about. She wrote her memoirs, entitled *My Life's History,* in 1952. Her one-hundredth birthday was declared Grandma Moses Day by then New York Governor Nelson Rockefeller.

American painter, sculptor, and writer Frederic Remington is famous for his depiction of the American West. He was the son of Clara Sackrider and Seth Remington, a newspaper publisher. Remington was born in Canton, New York. His father enlisted in the Union Army during the Civil War, when Frederic was only a baby, and returned home a colonel when Remington was four years old. His father's constant tales and exploits always fascinated him.

He began sketching at age ten, and the next year, his family moved to Ogdensburg. There his interest in drawing increased as he portrayed frontier clashes between the Cavalry and American Indians. At fourteen, he painted an account of Roman warfare, copied from one of his schoolbooks, on a discarded window shade. He attended the Highland Military Academy in Massachusetts and then Yale in 1878, where he studied art.

The academic study of art did not interest him, and he began to do journalistic cartoons for the Yale newspaper *Courant*.

He left school and then spent much of his time travelling across the United States on horseback, working as a hired cowboy, prospecting for gold, and holding other odd jobs. He recorded the lifestyle in art. He began submitting his drawings to magazines in 1882, when he was accepted by *Harper's Weekly*, which encouraged him to become a pictorial historian of the American West.

His second picture of the West was not published until 1885, and he then moved to New York to establish an art career. Many editors of magazines were reluctant to print pictures of the Wild West, preferring to give their readers the impression that the country was a peaceful respite from city life. *Harper's Weekly* accepted a third picture from him in 1886 and ran it on the cover, the first to appear exclusively as his own. His other submissions were re-drawn by a "professional" on staff at the magazine.

He then received recognition by the conservative National Academy of Design with his work *The Courier's Nap on the Trail* (1887?). Remington began to create clay models of his subjects in 1895. *Bronco Buster* (1895) demonstrates his unique technical skill of suspending figures on slim supports, such as a person on a horse, which is supported by its hooves. In 1896, he got a job as an artist and correspondent in Cuba with the *New York Journal*, owned by William R. Hearst.

Always ambitious, Remington began to write and published the illustrated books *Pony Tracks, Men with the Bark On,* and *The Way of an Indian*. Remington received a note from then-colonel Theodore Roosevelt stating, "You come closer to the real thing with the pen than any other man in the Western business."

Frederic Remington

The son of a saddle shop owner, Paul Signac (SEEN-yock), born on November 11, 1863, was a leading figure in the neo-impressionist school known for the technique pointillism, also referred to as divisionism. Signac took an early interest in art while visiting the various art dealers along the avenue on his way to school. It's been told that once he was sketching an Edgar Degas (see no. 47) painting at a gallery and was thrown out of the gallery by Paul Gauguin (see no. 55) for doing so.

Signac's taste was always for impressionism, which favored bright colors and painting directly from nature. To overtly express his views, he named his boat *Manet-Zola-Wagner* for the three most controversial names in art, literature, and music of the time. In Signac's opinion, an impressionist painter strove to become a "non-conformist, revolutionary, and make a virtue out of enjoying life."

In 1884, he met the pointillist painter Georges Seurat (see no. 57), with whom he formed a close friendship. He then participated in the founding of the Salon des Indepéndants, organized by artists rejected from exhibiting at the official Salon in France.

Signac then developed his own style of pointillism, described as a juxtaposition of dots using pure color. The dots created an effect similar to that produced by the refraction of light through a prism or a rainbow, lending his paintings the impression of glittering sunlight. He depicted nature and landscapes, most notably river scenes, and his most famous work is *Port St. Tropez* (1889).

Seurat's death in 1891 was a severe shock to Signac, who thought of Seurat as a mentor. It

Paul Signac

was the most serious period in his life, and he considered abandoning the fight of the impressionists. Recovering, he married Berthe Robles, a relative of the painter Camille Pissarro (see no. 44). He later published his views of the art world in the book titled *From Delacroix to Neo-Impressionism* (1899).

By 1900, Signac had adopted the use of small squares of color in painting to produce a mosaic effect, best depicted in the work *View of Port Marseilles* (1905). From 1908 to 1934, he went on to become president of the Salon des Indepéndants and exhibited the works of cubist artists and controversial fauves, a term meaning "wild beast" and applied for the fauves' use of bright colors.

Signac's life was spent opposing conventional rules. He died on August 15, 1935.

EDVARD MUNCH
(1863–1944)

Edvard Munch

studied under Christian Krohg. He was then awarded a state grant to study in Paris when he was twenty-two years old. While in France, he was influenced by impressionist works, especially those of Paul Gauguin (see no. 55) and Henri de Toulouse-Lautrec (see no. 62). At that time, Munch became associated with a new lifestyle, labeled as bohemian. In 1892, Munch was invited to exhibit at the Union of Berlin Artists in Germany. The exhibit opened and closed within a week, due to the controversy created by the violent emotion depicted in Munch's work. The "Munch Affair" was debated in the press and further raised unanswered questions about artistic freedom of expression.

Simultaneously, he painted stage sets for several of Ibsen's (1828–1906) plays. Henrik Ibsen was among the several writers included in Munch's circle of friends. Between 1892 and 1908, Munch travelled frequently between Paris and Berlin. He continued to paint frantically, and he also began to make prints using etching and woodcuts, showing the anxiety of human existence.

The emotional power of his works made him one of the most noted figures in the early development of modern art. His most celebrated painting, the world-famous *The Scream* or *The Cry* (1893), is typical of the expression of isolation and fear included in his works. Pessimistic in his portrayal of misery, illness, and death, such as in the works *Dead Life* (1900) and *Dead Mother* (1900), Munch challenged conventional views of life and death by invoking a sense of passion in natural causes. He spent his last years in solitude, painting in a more colorful and less pessimistic manner with an increased interest in nature.

At the age of seventeen, Edvard Munch (MOONK) began to paint pictures to express his personal grief after the death of his mother and older sister from tuberculosis. His father and brother also died when he was young, and another sister was institutionalized in a psychiatric hospital. He resolved to paint the states of mind of "living people who breathe and feel and suffer and love." The spectacle of death was a principal theme in his work, such as *The Sick Child* (1886) and *The Death Chamber* (1892).

Born on December 12, 1863 in Loten, Norway, Munch showed an aptitude for drawing at an early age. He attended the School of Art and Handcraft in Oslo, Norway, where he

Known in his family as the "little treasure" because of his spirited nature, Henri de Toulouse-Lautrec (too-LOOSE-low-TREK) was energetic and passionate about life, even after two accidents crippled him for life. A fall on a polished floor when he was fourteen years old caused him to break a leg, while a fall in a ditch in 1879 caused him to break his other leg. The falls left his legs weak, and they stopped growing. As an adult, he was only four and a half feet tall. Born on November 24, 1864, in Albi, France, Henri-Marie-Raymond de Toulouse-Lautrec came from a family that claimed descent from nobility, but the story was a myth. Toulouse-Lautrec's mother, Adèle Tapié de Céleyran, was first cousin to his father, Count Alphonese, as he called himself. His father was a gambler and flirt with a passion for colorful and flamboyant clothing, whom Toulouse-Lautrec depicted in an unflattering way in many portraits.

In addition to his short stature, Toulouse-Lautrec was also inflicted with a speech impediment, which made him pronounce the "s" sound like a "t" sound. Although he had some physical challenges, he made caricatures of himself in a humorous way.

His earliest memory of drawing was at age three, when he signed the register at a christening in a church with a picture of an ox. At age sixteen, he began to draw seriously, especially horses and everything associated with them. He possessed a natural skill to depict movement. His family encouraged his artistic pursuit and engaged a family friend to instruct him. In 1882, after the divorce of his parents, he went to live with his mother in Paris and became a student of León Bonnat, who was an accredited portrait painter of statesmen and philosophers.

Interested in painting the artificial, ornamental, and the spectacular, he had an aversion to painting landscapes, stating that "the human figure is all that counts." He lived enthusiastically in the Montmarte section of Paris. There he would visit cafes, dance halls, cabarets, and the theater, sketching his surroundings, then expanding them into bright color paintings. It was also at this time that he was inspired by the art of James Whistler (see no. 46), and he was taught by Edgar Degas (see no. 47) to paint "as if he were looking through the keyhole," so that the model appeared unaware of the presence of the artist. His passion for the eccentric and ostentatious led him to drink heavily, which eventually affected his health. In 1891, he produced the first of many posters, *La Goulue at the Moulin Rouge*, demonstrating his affection for flamboyant scenes. Since his death on September 9, 1901, the collection of Moulin Rouge posters have been in high demand.

Henri de Toulouse-Lautrec

63. CAMILLE CLAUDEL
(1864–1943)

Camille Claudel

Camille Claudel (cloe-DELL) began to work with clay as a child, although nothing in her history indicated an artistic background. She was born at Fere-en-tardenuis on December 8, 1864, to parents who did little to encourage and support one another or their children. Apparently, according to her brother Paul Claudel (1868–1955), who was later to become a famous writer, "Everyone always fought in the family."

Educated at the Colarossi Academy in Paris, Claudel began her career as a sculptor at age twenty, apprenticed to Auguste Rodin (see no. 49), who was forty years old at the time. Exhibiting natural talent, she eventually became a collaborator of Rodin and assisted him in a variety of projects, including the famous *Gates of Hell* (1880). Soon after, she became his mistress. Her work was intertwined with his, concentrating on busts and naked figure groups in contorted poses. Demonstrating her lyrical and sensitive style, she also continued to do her own work, including a famous bronze statue *Young Girl with a Sheaf* (1890).

Continuing to live with her parents, who disapproved of her relationship with Rodin, she eventually moved to her own apartment in 1888, near Rodin's studio. Four years later, her relationship with him began to deteriorate. Having contributed whole figures and parts of figures to Rodin's projects, she felt used by him—especially as his reputation grew and she remained relatively obscure.

From 1892 on, she worked on her own and refused to exhibit her work with Rodin. Although she exhibited at reputable showings, such as the Salon des Indépendants and Salon d'Automne, her work did not sell. She was also known to destroy sculptures she produced, outraged by Rodin's supposed injustice to her.

At age forty-nine, she was committed to the first of several psychiatric hospitals, and she remained a psychiatric patient for many years until her death. Her letters to her brother are a testament to her disappointments in life. Her work remained obscure until it had a resurgence during the 1970s and 1980s, and her story was immortalized in the film *Camille Claudel* (1988).

All his life, American photographer Alfred Stieglitz (STEEG-lits) took pride in doing things his own way, ignoring rules he considered to be unreasonable and inventing ones that suited him. Born on January 1, 1864, he was the oldest of six children of Edward Stieglitz, an immigrant to New York City from Germany, who made a living as a wool merchant.

In 1881, his father retired and the family moved to Germany where Stieglitz enrolled at the Berlin Polytechnic Institute. He first studied mechanical engineering but shifted to photography and chemistry, which interested him more.

Stieglitz returned to the United States when he was twenty-six years old and went to work at the Helichrome Engraving Company, a photo engraving firm. Maintaining an interest in photography, he edited the magazine *American Amateur Photographer* from 1891 to 1896, and he was the editor of the magazine *Camera Notes* from 1897 to 1902.

Stieglitz's photographs are characterized by their candor and realism, lending an element of purity and simplicity. Stieglitz never defined his work other than through pure technical explanations, such as the use of lighting, allowing the viewer to draw a personal conclusion on the subject matter and the feelings portrayed. *Venetian Boy* (1887), a picture of a ten-year-old street urchin, communicates the capacity for humankind to sustain suffering and still remain beautiful.

His other famous photographs include *The Terminal* (1892), which shows a conductor of a horse-drawn streetcar taking a rest, and *Night* (1896), described by him as an attempt to make a clear picture of a dark street.

In 1902, along with Edward Steichen (1879–1973), Stieglitz founded the Photo Secession, an organization of pictorial photographers. The group produced the magazine *Camera Work*, published from 1903 until 1917. The group also opened their own gallery, officially named Little Galleries of the Photo Secession. Due to its location at 291 Fifth Avenue in New York City, it came to be called 291. He used the gallery to introduce to the public the works of European and American artists, such as Pablo Picasso (see no. 71) and Georgia O'Keeffe (see no. 81). Stieglitz married O'Keeffe in 1924 and created a series of photographs of her; they are considered his greatest works.

Gallery 291 closed in 1917, but Stieglitz opened two other galleries between 1925 and 1929. Stieglitz was the first to exhibit photographs in major museums across the United States and the first to make photography recognized as an art form. He died on July 13, 1946.

Alfred Stieglitz

Robert Henry Cozad, better known as Robert Henri, was the mentor of the group of painters known as the Eight, or the Ashcan School. Founded in 1908, Henri and his colleagues broke with academic tradition and conservative standards to paint American life with dramatic realism. He was born on June 24, 1865, in Cincinnati, Ohio. As a boy, his family adopted separate last names and Henri was passed off as a foster child. The family was forced to live as fugitives after Henri's father killed a man in self-defense.

After attending the Pennsylvania Academy of Fine Arts in Philadelphia, he left for Paris in 1888 to attend the Academie Julian and the Ecole des Beaux-Arts, the official art academy.

Returning to the United States in 1900, he began a long career as a teacher, first at the New York School of Art until 1909, then at his private school in New York until 1915, when he began to teach at the Art Students League. Among his students were George Bellows (see no. 73) and Edward Hopper (see no. 75).

Henri taught that any subject taken from life was suitable to paint. A compilation of his lectures, entitled *The Art Spirit*, was published in 1923. Renowned for his dark colors and broad brush strokes, Henri and his colleagues took as their subject matter slum areas, low-class restaurants, working-class people, littered streets, and similar scenes, which earned them the name Ashcan School. Henri's most celebrated works are *Laughing Boy* (1907), *Young Woman in Black* (1907), and *Portrait of Mrs. Robert Henri* (1911).

In 1910, he organized the Independent Artist Exhibition. It did not have a jury of panelists deciding which artists were suitable to exhibit there. The show championed the cause of independent artists and established a new liberal position on art.

Robert Henri

66. WASSILY KANDINSKY
(1866–1944)

As an artist and a theorist, Russian painter Wassily Kandinsky played an important role in the development of abstract art. He used spontaneous shapes and squiggles to symbolize ideas and intangible states of thought. After visiting a French impressionist exhibit, where he viewed the works of Claude Monet (see no. 50), Kandinsky decided to pursue a career as an artist. Born in Moscow on December 4, 1866, he was nearly thirty years old when he left an academic law career to study drawing, sketching, and anatomy in Germany under Anton Azbe and at the Munich Academy with Franz von Stuck.

Learning to play the piano and cello as a child influenced his paintings later on, including the titles he gave to his works. Kandinsky's art was more abstract than the art pioneered by the impressionists. Kandinsky's painting made no references to real objects. Demonstrating great talent early on, he began to exhibit throughout Europe, defining his form of art both on canvas and in writing. Kandinsky travelled widely from 1900 to 1910. He came in contact with the art of Paul Gauguin (see no. 55), neo-impressionist paintings, and the paintings of les fauves artists, who were known for their use of brilliant colors.

In 1911, Kandinsky formed the group known as The Blue Rider (Der Blaue Reiter) with other expressionist artists including Franz Marc and Paul Klee (see no. 70). The group produced art that was characterized by complex patterns and brilliant colors, especially blue. In 1912, Kandinsky published *Concerning the Spiritual in Art*, the first theoretical views on abstract art. Forever inventing new forms of geometric shapes, Kandinsky was invited to teach in Moscow from 1918 to 1921 and later at the famed Bauhaus School of Art in Dessau, Germany, from 1922 to 1933.

Relocating to Paris after the German government shut down the Bauhaus as a perpetrator of "degenerate" thought, Kandinsky met the artist Joan Miró (see no. 84), who further influenced his work. *Composition VIII No. 260* (1923) exemplifies his ideas with a composition of lines, circles, arcs, and simple geometric forms. *Swinging* (1925) depicts colored shapes arranged on a canvas to suggest movement, while the colors create a sense of space in the painting.

Kandinsky painted until his death in Paris on December 13, 1944. He is classified as one of the first explorers of non-representational, abstract art. The majority of his art was purchased by collector Solomon Guggenheim, who exhibited the paintings in his New York art museum.

Wassily Kandinsky

67. GUTZON BORGLUM
(1867–1941)

Gutzon de la Mothe Borglum was a man of great imagination. An American sculptor, he was known for his political statues carved into natural rock formations.

Born in Bear Lake, Idaho, and raised in Nebraska, Borglum attempted on several occasions to write his autobiography, but he never completed the project. The main point stressed in his notes was possessing the courage to be oneself without the need for popular approval. Appropriately, his middle name, de la Mothe, means "the one with courage" in French.

As a child, education was stressed in the house, and Borglum was sent to St. Mary's College in Kansas, where he learned to draw. After he completed school, the family moved to California, where Borglum went to work as a lithographer, learning to engrave and design on stone.

After painting *Stage Coach* (1887?), noted for its realism and detail of expression, he was discovered by a local art collector who purchased his work, allowing him the opportunity to travel to Paris and study at the Ecole des Beaux-Arts. His break came in 1891, when a delivery man mistakenly brought a bronze statue of his, *Death of the Chief*, to the Salon, the government-sponsored art gallery, and it was immediately accepted. The honor allowed him the opportunity to meet the sculptor Auguste Rodin (see no. 49).

In 1916, Borglum was commissioned by a group of Southern women to execute an image of General Robert E. Lee (1807–1870) for the face of Stone Mountain in Georgia. While the women had planned for an isolated figure, he envisioned a full regalia of figures. Dissension soon occurred as expenses grew; he destroyed the models, and the state of Georgia filed a lawsuit. Borglum won the case, but he was dismissed from the project.

In 1927, he was commissioned by the United States government to execute his most famous work, the Mount Rushmore sculpture in South Dakota. He choose the four presidents, George Washington, Thomas Jefferson, Abraham Lincoln, and Theodore Roosevelt, for their ideas on American land expansionism and political development of the country. Carved into the mountain 500 feet (152 m) above the ground, each head is 70 feet (21 m) high. The massive heads were carved with dynamite and jackhammers. Borglum's ability to create sculptures on a grand scale defined him as an engineer as well as an artist, making his contributions a combination of technical and artistic mastery. He dedicated the last fourteen years of his life to carving Mount Rushmore. Upon his death, his son Lincoln completed the project. The work cost over one million dollars to complete. Other large scale works of Borglum's include *The Mares of Diomedes'* and the head of *Abraham Lincoln* in the U.S. Capitol Rotunda.

Gutzon Borglum

French painter, sculptor, and lithographer Henri Emile Benoit Matisse (mah-TEESE) was regarded as a master in the use of color and form to convey emotion. He was born on December 31, 1869, to a middle-class family in the industrial town of Le Cateau-Cambrésis, France. At age eighteen, he was sent to Paris to study law. Two years later, suffering from an attack of appendicitis, he began to paint to pass the time while recovering. Reading a how-to-paint book by Frederic Goupil, Matisse later enrolled in a local drawing class, continuing to work at a law office. Realizing that his double life was intolerable, Matisse quit law and went to Paris to enroll in the Ecole des Beaux-Arts, where he was first taught by Adolphe Bouguereau and then Gustave Moreau (see no. 42). Matisse began to methodically copy art from the masters he saw at the Louvre museum, following exact detail without adding any personal style. Not until he was twenty-seven years old did he really begin to paint, after discovering some of the more radical artists of the time.

When Matisse was thirty, Moreau had died, and Matisse began to experiment with impressionism. His new instructor, Eugène Carrière, did not approve of Matisse's new style. His first painting incorporating bright colors, *Still Life Against the Light of 1899* (1899), was met with controversy at the school.

Developing the use of color to depict structure, the public first viewed Matisse's work at the 1905 Salon d'Automne. The portrait of his wife, *Woman with the Hat* (1905?), was abused by critics for its "formless confusion of colors." Matisse and others using that style were labeled les fauves, French for "wild beast."

Matisse travelled to Africa the year after the show and was the first to incorporate its culture and landscape into art. The painting *Blue Nude* (1906) emphasizes his use of the three

Henri Matisse

dimensional aspect of the figure.

His success grew among foreign patrons, including writer Gertrude Stein. He broke with les fauves in 1907 and never belonged to another identifiable movement. A year later, he opened his own art school in France, which he operated for three years. In 1913, he was accepted to exhibit at the New York Armory Show, which introduced European art to the American public. In New York, people were surprised to meet him, expecting an ill-dressed, uneducated man, judging from his paintings.

After World War I, he began to design sets for Sergei Diaghilev's ballets. Other experiments in art included illustrations for books, such as *Poésies de Stephen Mallarmé* (1932) and a series of works using shapes cut from brightly colored paper.

He continued to paint into old age, producing *Egyptian Curtain* (1948) and *Large Interior in Red* (1949?). Matisse died on November 3, 1954.

Georges Rouault

Widely exhibited and highly respected in his lifetime, Georges Henri Rouault (roo-OH) was a French painter devoted to depicting religious themes. The son of a cabinet maker, Rouault was born on May 27, 1871, in a cellar shelter during an artillery shelling of Paris at the time of the Commune Revolt. Rouault began an artistic career at age fourteen, when he was apprenticed to a maker of stained glass. A profound love for art manifested itself in him. When sent on errands, he would save the bus fare to buy paint.

At age nineteen, he entered the Ecole des Beaux-Arts school of art and studied under Gustave Moreau (see no. 42), later forming part of les fauve group, meaning "wild beasts" for their use of vibrant colors. He left the school five years later after two unsuccessful attempts to win the Prix de Rome competition. The death of Moreau left him depressed. Rouault began to paint subjects concerning the human conditions of immorality and redemption. At this time, he formed a friendship with the Catholic writer Leon Bloy, who heavily influenced his work. In 1903, 1904, and 1905, he exhibited at the Salon d'Automne with representations of clowns, circus people, and street people. The public rejected the dark mood and tone of his works, which reflected anger and sadness for the plight of humanity.

At thirty-nine, he had his first solo show at the Galerie Druet in Paris, which succeeded in attracting the interest of the critics. On his way to fame, he met the art dealer and publisher Ambroise Vollard, with whom he signed a contract in 1917, allowing Vollard to purchase all his unfinished work. Among the paintings executed during this period were *The Old Clown* (1917) and *The Lovely Madame X* (1915), which was a satire on the indifference of the upper class to World War I. Rouault also created prints, the most notable collection being *Misere* (1914).

After Vollard's death, Rouault was tied to legal battles to recover over eight hundred unfinished paintings. He retrieved most of them and burned 315 that he felt he would not be able to finish or did not want to finish.

Around 1928, he heralded a new painting style likened to stained glass windows. The paintings demonstrating this style are *Christ Mocked by Soldiers* (1932) and *Head of Christ* (1938). Rouault did not travel until 1948, when he made his first trip to Italy. Although he did not show his work while employed by Vollard, he did publish articles and poetry under the title *Souvenirs Intimes*.

In 1951, he was designated Commander of the Legion of Honor, a society of acclaimed artists officially recognized by the state. Two years later, Pope Pius XII appointed him a papal knight. Upon his death, Rouault was given a state funeral, the first ever given to an artist by the French government.

70. PAUL KLEE
(1879–1940)

Belonging to no specific art movement, Paul Klee, a Swiss painter and watercolorist who was known for fantastic dream images and use of color, was an individualist, remaining aloof from all artistic alliances. The landscape that surrounded him as a youth provided a natural medieval flair that allowed him to combine the grotesque and the fairy tale in his art, which he labeled with fantastic poetic titles, such as *Two Men Meet, Each Believing the Other to Be of Higher Rank* (1903).

Klee was born on December 18, 1879, near Bern, Switzerland. His parents were musicians who instilled in him a love of music. An accomplished violinist, Klee linked music to art. At nineteen years of age, he moved to Munich, Germany, where he studied at the Munich Academy and apprenticed with the painter Franz von Stuck. At that time, he made his first trip to Italy. When Klee was thirty-two years old, he met members of The Blue Rider (Der Blaue Reiter) group, established by Kandinsky (see no. 66) as a rebellion against impressionism and a promotion of abstract art. Klee exhibited with The Blue Rider group in their second showing, even though he never became an official member.

His earliest works were pencil landscapes that showed the influence of impressionism. Klee was a master draftsman, and he did many elaborate line drawings using dream imagery as subject matter. He described his technique in the drawings as "taking a line for a walk." He incorporated letters and numbers into his work; they were used to create a medium between the abstract and real, as in *Once Emerged from the Gray of Night* (1918).

A trip to Tunisia, Africa, in 1914 moved him toward using color and marked the beginning of his fully mature style, in which he declared himself "a true painter . . . possessed by color." The piece that commemorates this period in his art was a composition of colored

Paul Klee

squares entitled *Red and White Domes* (1914).

Klee believed that "art does not reproduce the visible, rather it makes the visible," because he considered the process of forming more significant than the final form. He taught at the Bauhaus School from 1920 to 1931 and published an essay on art theory in 1925. In 1931, he began teaching at the Dusseldorf Academy but was soon dismissed by the Nazis, who said his art was "degenerate."

In 1933, he returned to Switzerland and developed a crippling skin disease known as scleroderma. During this time, his subject matter grew increasingly gloomy. His last painting, *Still Life* (1940), is a summation of his lifelong concern as an artist, that "the objective world surrounding us is not the only one possible; there are others latent."

Pablo Picasso

One of the most prolific artists in history, the Spanish painter and sculptor Pablo Picasso created more than twenty thousand works in his lifetime. Born on October 25, 1881, in Malága, Spain, Picasso was the son of an art teacher, José Ruiz Blasco. Picasso was first taught to paint by his father.

The diversity of Picasso's art, which art historians divide into periods, prompted the remark by writer Georges Dessaignes, "Nothing that anyone can say about Picasso is correct." Picasso's first painting, *Picador*, was completed when he was eight years old and depicted a bullfight. His genius lies in the fact that he experimented with every medium of art. In his own words, "The whole world is open before us, everything waiting to be done."

By age nineteen, Picasso was dividing his time between France and Spain, working in different styles of painting until his development of cubism, in collaboration with Georges Braque (see no. 74). Depicting beggars and the bohemian street life of Paris, Picasso's Blue Period, dating from 1901 to 1904, was so termed for the melancholy subject matter and cool blue tones. Blindness was a characteristic depicted in most of his subjects of this time, denoting a inner vision, such as in *The Old Guitarist* (1903).

Following this was the Rose Period, named for the pink shades. The subjects during this period were dancers, acrobats, and harlequins. The break from lyrical painting occurred in 1906, when Picasso was influenced by African art, as seen in *Les Demoiselles d'Avignon* (1907). The painting shocked the public with its stark, primitive exposure of the female form, distorted into geometric shapes, later termed cubism. Cubism attempted to interpret a three-dimensional world on a two-dimensional canvas by destroying the continuity of the surface and reducing the subject to sharp-edged planes.

Multiple views of any given object, musical instruments being his favorite, were superimposed to present the idea of the structure of the object and its position in space. Picasso's most famous cubist paintings were *Head of a Woman* (1909) and *The Three Musicians* (1921).

Continuing to test the art world, he created the art form known as collage when he pasted an oilcloth to the painting *Still Life with Chair—Caning* (1912). Picasso applied the principle of cubism to sculpture, as in *Mandolin and Clarinet* (1914). The work dating from 1918 to 1925, developing the cubist technique, was later termed the Classical Period.

Experiencing personal turmoil, his mood coincided with the outbreak of the Spanish Civil War, moving him to paint *Guernica* (1937). A grim portrayal of the horrors of war, the painting displays a complexity of symbolism to express his feelings. In 1971, this large work was exhibited at the Louvre museum in Paris, making Picasso the only living artist to show there. He died on April 8, 1973 in Mougins, France.

An Italian painter and sculptor who was a leader of the futurist movement, Umberto Boccioni (botch-ee-OWN-ee) wrote the *Technical Manifesto of Futuristic Painting* (1910), urging artists to abandon the constraints of enclosed space and adopt technological civilization. Born in Calabria, Italy, on October 19, 1882, he visited Rome when he was sixteen years old, where he began studying art with Giacomo Balla, who turned his style toward neo-impressionism. Balla encouraged him to venture into new art media and introduced him to the color theories applied by the neo-impressionists.

After visiting France and Russia, Boccioni settled in Milan, Italy, in 1908, where he was employed as a commercial artist. It was at this time that he met the writer Filippo Tommaso Marinetti, author of *Foundation and Manifesto of Futurism*, who demanded that new art should be based on the dynamic element of life, namely speed. Following Marinetti's belief that Italian culture was burdened by a past that prohibited progress, Boccioni joined the group of futurist painters and became an ardent speaker for the group. He also became a principal theorist in mobile sculptures to create a sense of movement, believing that artists should express the vitality of industrialization in their work.

As with most futurist painters, the continuous movement of planes in space was an obsession with Boccioni. His revolutionary vision of art was best paraphrased by his comment, "Let us open the figure like a window and include in it the milieu in which it lives." In painting, Boccioni would distort forms into a spectrum of colors to create a link between space and solid objects. He labeled the sense of action in painting and sculpture "dynamic abstraction." His first major futuristic work was *The City Rises* (1909), which demonstrated the growth of the modern industrial city and the people living in it.

After 1911, he was introduced to cubism, influencing his later work. Three years later, he published his book *Futuristic Paintings and Sculptures (Pittura-scultura futurista)*. In 1912, he advocated the use of a motor to create movement in the planes and lines of his sculptures. Examples of this are *State of Mind* (1911) and *Forces of a Street* (1911).

Continuously adding to the forms and styles of art that he was introduced to, Boccioni incorporated glass and cement into his sculptures, breaking away from traditional material. The importance he placed in the combination of material and the space around an object is exemplified in his piece *Development of a Bottle in Space* (1912). In 1915, he volunteered for military service in World War I, and in 1916, while recovering from a wound, he was killed in a riding accident.

Umberto Boccioni

George Bellows

American realist painter George Wesley Bellows distinguished himself as an artist in his youth. Born in Columbus, Ohio, on August 19, 1882, he received his first instruction in art at Ohio State University, where he also contributed cartoons to the student paper. Before graduating in 1904, he left the university to enroll at the New York School of Art. Taught by the painter Robert Henri (see no. 65), he began to paint scenes of poverty and destitution, entirely new to American art at the time.

He became determined to create art based on the unique character of life in the United States. Although associated with the group known as The Eight, or Ashcan School, which was headed by Henri, Bellows maintained independence in his art by using references to the classics in his work. By 1907, he had begun

to attract public attention with his paintings on the sport of boxing, including *A Knockout* and *Club Night* (1907), which incorporated his past desire to have excelled in sports into his art. Two years later, he painted *Stag Night at Sharkey's* (1909), which was described as having a revolutionary style incorporating liquidity of movement.

Despite his identification with The Eight, and partly for his accomplished landscape paintings, he was elected an associate of the National Academy at age twenty-seven, becoming the youngest artist to receive the recognition. Four years later, he was elected a full member. His paintings had universal appeal to a mass public, as he was also fascinated by the spectacle of people and buildings in the city. In 1913, he was one of the American artists represented at the New York Armory Show, which introduced European art to Americans.

At twenty-eight years of age, he married and began a teaching career at the Art Students League in New York City. Branching out to lithography in 1916, he made over two hundred prints of various city scenes, literary illustrations, and satirical commentaries. Disturbed by the events of World War I, he recorded his emotions in a series of prints which were often compared to the work of the artist Francisco de Goya (see no. 33), due to Bellows's technique that applied a geometric system of quantifying the relationship of color.

By 1919, he was teaching at the Chicago Art Institute and completing illustrations for novels by author H. G. Wells. Representing both the avant-garde and the classical tradition in his paintings, he was revered for his innovative style and subject matter.

Following in his father's profession, Georges Braque (BROCK), born on May 13, 1882, apprenticed himself to the house-painting and decorating business at age seventeen. Raised in the French seaport town of Le Havre on the English Channel, he always had an affinity for the landscape. Working for his father and other local decorators, he gained an understanding of materials, craftsmanship, and decorative effects. Moving to Paris at eighteen, he enrolled in evening art classes, but continued to work as a decorator, still not convinced that he could become a professional painter. He experimented with several art schools and visited the Louvre museum often to view the works of the masters.

After seeing a series of exhibits by the painter Paul Cezanne (see no. 48), Braque established a studio for himself and began to paint seriously. In 1906, he showed his first paintings at the Salon des Indépendants, following the les fauve style of vibrant colors. He later destroyed all of these paintings. He met the artist Pablo Picasso (see no. 71), and they began their interpretation of nature through "cylinders, spheres, and cones." Art historians consider this to be the origin of cubist paintings. Two of Braque's best-known works of this period are *House at L'Estaque* (1908) and *Road Near L'Estaque* (1908). In 1908, a critic published an article in the magazine *Gil Blas* accusing Braque of "reducing everything to little cubes." Braque and Picasso, who were now collaborating in art, were concerned with creating a "tactile space" that is essentially the use of a two-dimensional picture surface as opposed to the illusion of three-dimensional objects.

Braque's most famous painting during his time with Picasso was *Violin and Candlestick* (1910). Although his work was controversial, it received international acclaim. In 1912, he and Picasso invented the collage style of art. Braque pasted strips of wallpaper onto painted canvas-

Georges Braque

es and created fifty-seven of these collages, including *Still Life on a Table: Gillette* (1914) and *The Violin* (1914).

Drafted into the French army in 1914, he served for three years and received a severe head wound. Upon his return to Paris, his partnership with Picasso had ended, and he adopted a more sensuous style. Braque did not have his major retrospective exhibit until 1933, in Basel, Switzerland.

After World War II, he took an interest in Eastern mysticism, especially Zen Buddhism. His later paintings suggest a quest for the spiritual, and images of birds in flight dominated his works in the 1950s and 1960s. Braque produced sculptures, graphics, book illustrations, and decorative art. He continued to work until his death on August 31, 1963.

With a wide reputation as the artist who painted the loneliness and boredom of city life, Edward Hopper is revered as the epitome of American realist painters. Embarking on a artistic career in New York, where he was born on July 22, 1882, he studied illustration in a commercial art school at age seventeen. Two years later, he switched to painting and enrolled at the New York School of Art, taught by Robert Henri (see no. 65). Between 1906 and 1910, he made four trips to Europe, which exposed him to different art styles but did not influence his own.

On his return to the United States, he abandoned painting to continue a career as a commercial illustrator. He exhibited only once, at the 1913 Armory Show in New York, which presented "modern art" from Europe and the United States. He did not paint seriously again until he was forty-one years old.

He married Josephine Nivison, an artist in her own right, in 1924. In one of her shows, she exhibited some of his works, including *House by the Railroad* (1925), which helped further his career. It was during this time that he stated, "I don't think I ever tried to paint the American scene; I'm trying to paint myself." His paintings had a composition style based on simple geometric forms, flat masses of color, and the use of architectural elements to create blunt shapes and angles.

The figures in his works were all isolated, anonymous, and non-communicative, as portrayed best in the famous *Nighthawks* (1942). The painting shows an all-night cafe, where the few customers are illuminated by the eerie glare of electric lights.

Hopper's sense of loneliness was rooted in his presentation of familiar city scenes and concrete subjects, such as barren apartments, lunch counters, and city streets. In landscapes, he depicted America as an alienating and vacuous space. The figures in all his works appear despairing and alone. He earned widespread recognition for providing visual form to the emotions of the big city. Considered revolutionary in art, he characterized the sense of human hopelessness, also indicative of the time of the Great Depression of the 1930s. Among his works of that time were *Room in Brooklyn* (1932) and *Cape Cod Evening* (1939).

Hopper's style was influential in the development of pop art later. His style and subject matter, characterized by melancholy, remained unchanged throughout his life.

Edward Hopper

IMOGEN CUNNINGHAM
(1883–1976)

An American photographer best known for her realistic portraits and closeups of flowers and plants, Imogen Cunningham began taking pictures in 1906 with a small-format camera acquired from a mail-order correspondence school.

She was the daughter of Isaac and Susan Cunningham of Portland, Oregon. The family moved to Seattle, Washington, when Imogen was six years old. She entered the University of Washington in 1903, majoring in chemistry. After viewing a photography exhibit of Gertrude Kasebier, she wrote a thesis on *The Scientific Development of Photography* and decided to pursue a career in photography. After working in a portrait studio, learning to retouch negatives and print with platinum paper, she traveled to Dresden, Germany, to study photographic chemistry. At twenty-seven, she published her research on substituting lead salts for platinum in photographic print paper. The publication was followed by a thesis entitled *Photography as a Profession for Women*.

Amazingly active, she had her first solo exhibition in 1914 at the Brooklyn Institute of Arts and Sciences in New York, showing works such as *Marsh at Dawn* (1901), which imitated the academic painting of romanticism, and the allegorical prints entitled *The Woods Beyond the World* (1912). The next year, she married Roi Partridge, a photographer in his own right, with whom she had three sons. The couple settled in the San Francisco Bay area of California, where she began a commercial portrait business in 1921. Being a mother confined her to the house much of the time, and she began to photograph the objects around her. Plant forms and flowers were the most accessible subjects, especially since she also had a passion for gardening. Joining an association of West Coast photographers known as Group f.64, who rejected the popular sentimental photography of the time, she began to show her work in museums throughout California. Her photographs were famous for their sharp focus, such as *Two Callas* (1929).

Divorced in 1934, she changed her style to documentary street photography and soon began to take pictures with a 35mm camera. Included in exhibitions around the world, she traveled extensively to Europe. Upon her return to the United States, she supplemented her art career by taking teaching positions periodically at the San Francisco Art Institute. Recognized internationally, she was also featured in the film *Two Photographers* by Fred Padula in 1966, and ten years later, she was profiled in a documentary by CBS television.

Imogen Cunningham

German expressionist painter and print-maker Max Beckmann, born on February 12, 1884, was famous for his pessimistic portrayal of society and catastrophic events, such as the sinking of the ship *Titanic* in 1912. The son of a prosperous flour business owner, Beckmann entered the Art Academy at Dresden, Germany, at age fifteen. He was expelled soon after for exhibiting too much independence in his work. Entering the Weimar Academy, where he received a traditional art training, he won a scholarship to study in Paris at age nineteen. After a few weeks at the Paris Academy, he left, claiming, "What they do there, I already know." He walked the entire way from Paris to Berlin in order to "see things," he said.

Not long after his arrival, he married Minna Tube, a student at the Weimar Academy, whom he had met at a costume ball. Soon after the wedding, his mother died of cancer, which had a profound effect upon him and turned his work toward a depiction of pain and tragedy. That year, 1906, he painted the *Great Death Scene* to exorcise the shock of his mother's death. His art was now achieving great success, and in 1910, he was placed on the executive board of the renowned art group Berlin Secession. The office was normally reserved for artists twice his age. Beckmann resigned a year later to devote more time to his painting.

At thirty years of age, he enlisted in the medical corps of the German army during World War I. Although he meant to be an objective observer, he was discharged the following year for mental and physical exhaustion. After the experience, he settled in Frankfurt, Germany, where he proceeded to portray the horrifying experience of war. His work was characterized by heavy outlines, areas of harsh colors, and brutal subject matter. These pieces included *The Descent from the Cross* (1917) and *The Dream* (1921). He continued to express his feelings toward war into the 1930s, especially against the Nazi party. His painting *Departure* (1933) was a realistic allegory of figures in war. As a result of his outspoken attitude, he was dismissed from his professorship at the Stadel School of Arts. He emigrated to Amsterdam, Holland soon after. He finally settled in the United States in 1947, where he taught at Washington University in St. Louis, Missouri. He died on December 27, 1950.

Max Beckmann

78. DIEGO RIVERA
(1886–1957)

Diego Rivera inspired the movement of Mexican historical art with the depiction of social themes painted on murals for public buildings. He was born on December 8, 1886, in the former silver-mining town of Guanajuato, Mexico. Drawing since the age of three, Rivera first began his formal study of art at San Carlos Academy of Fine Arts at eleven years of age. Combining politics with art, he was heavily influenced by the folk art of José Posada, who painted satirical portraits criticizing the regime of the dictator Porfirio Diaz. Rivera commented that through Posada, he learned "that you cannot paint what you do not feel."

After five years at the academy, Rivera was expelled for leading a student strike against the re-election of Diaz. At sixteen years of age, Rivera defined himself as an independent artist, travelling and painting throughout the country. His most famous piece of this period was *The Threshing Floor* (1904), a depiction of realism. At twenty-one years of age, Rivera left for Spain to study. He was dissatisfied with the rigidity of the academic style in Spain, so from 1909 to 1920, he settled in France.

Rivera continued to take brief jaunts to England, Spain, and Holland, along with a return trip to Mexico in 1910 during the Mexican Revolution. He was introduced to the works of painters, including Paul Cezanne and Vincent van Gogh (see nos. 48 and 56).

Deciding that he was needed in the new revolutionary government in Mexico, Rivera returned in 1921. He joined the Mexican Communist Party and began to write for the official paper of the party, *El Machete*. In Mexico, he began to execute murals of Mexican social history, including festivals, industry, agriculture, and landscape. His first commission was 124 panels for the courtyard of the Ministry of Education, which took four years to complete. Two years later, in 1929, he

Diego Rivera

commenced his commemorative piece for the National Palace in Mexico City, painting an epic history of Mexico from pre-Columbian civilization to the present. The piece also included a forecast for the future. That year, he married the painter Frida Kahlo (see no. 94).

It was in New York in 1933 that he received the commission to decorate the lobby of the RCA building in Rockefeller Center. Rivera had painted the face of the Russian Bolshevik leader Vladimir Lenin on the mural, causing a scandal; the work was destroyed by authorities in 1934. Fortunately, one of his assistants had managed to photograph the piece before it was destroyed. He returned to Mexico and devoted his time to painting on canvas. Upon his death, Rivera was given a state funeral for his contribution to Mexico.

A French dada artist who focused on abstract dream imagery, Marcel Duchamp (doo-SHOMP) exerted a strong influence on the development of twentieth-century radical art. He came from an artistic family; his grandfather was an engraver and painter and his mother a musician. His brother, Gaston, abandoned a law career to become a painter under the name Jacques Villon. Another brother, Raymond Duchamp-Villon, left the medical profession to become a sculptor.

Born on July 28, 1887, in Blainville, Normandy, Duchamp painted his first oil painting, *Landscape at Blainville*, at age fifteen, and two years later, he left for Paris to study at the Académie Julian. Forced into military service soon after, he returned to Paris in 1904, where he began to draw cartoons for the magazines *Le Rire* and *Le Courrier Françis*. Continuing to explore different art movements, he was influenced by the rising fauve artists, who used vibrant colors, and in 1910, he painted *The Chess Players*, which depicted

Marcel Duchamp

members of his family as well as his fascination for the game. He followed the work with the *Nude Descending a Staircase* (1912), which was followed by the more famous *Nude Descending a Staircase No. 2* (1912). It demonstrated mechanical motion of the human figure in dozens of geometric shapes overlapping one another. He exhibited *Nude Descending a Staircase No. 2* at the Paris Salon des Indépendants in 1912, provoking anger from the other exhibiting artists. He quietly removed his painting.

At the 1913 Armory Show in New York, Duchamp again exhibited the painting, where one critic stated, "It looks like an explosion in a shingle factory." The experience ended Duchamp's serious involvement in painting. Taking a job as a library clerk, he did not exhibit but continued to paint. In 1913, he began to make his "ready-mades" in defiance of the laws of art. Ready-made art took objects out of a normal context and made an art form by simply showing them in a different way. An example of this type of art was the mounting of a bicycle tire upside down on a kitchen stool. The success of his ready-made art brought him to the United States in 1915, where he had a showing at the 291 gallery of the photographer Alfred Stieglitz (see no. 64).

After co-founding the Société Anonyme in New York City to promote modern art, Duchamp exhibited his controversial reproduction of the *Mona Lisa* by Leonardo da Vinci (see no. 9), to which he added a mustache and a goatee. The act was true to his goal of "annihilating painting." He continued working on his famous sculpture *The Bride Stripped Bare by Her Bachelors, Even*, also referred to as *Large Glass* (1923). The work is a construction of lead wire and painted foil on two glass plates. The irony was that his ready-mades, which were considered to be "anti-art," were being preserved in museums.

The oldest of nine children, Marc Chagall (sha-GAHL) was born on July 7, 1887, in Vitebsk, Russia. His father, who changed the family name from Segal to Chagall, financially supported his family by packing herring into barrels. His parents were both devout Hassidic Jews. Chagall began to copy illustrations from magazines as a boy and dreamed about a career in painting. His parents apprenticed him to a local photographer, thinking he would be better able to make a living as a photographer than a painter. Bored by retouching pictures, he persuaded his parents to allow him to study art. At twenty, he entered the Imperial School for the Protection of the Arts in St. Petersburg, Russia.

He worked as a sign painter to support himself. At this time, he painted *The Dead Man* (1898). The work depicts a funeral scene in his home town and also shows a man playing a fiddle on a rooftop. The theme later provided the source for the famous Broadway musical *Fiddler on the Roof*.

In 1910, Maxim Vinaver, a lawyer in St. Petersburg, saw Chagall's work and sponsored a trip to Paris for Chagall. There, Chagall developed a personal style that combined his memories of the small Russian village of his youth and the elements of fantasy. The two works indicative of this are *I and the Village* (1911) and *The Soldiers Drink* (1913).

Returning to Russia in 1916, he married Bella Rosenfeld, was appointed the cultural commissar of Vitebsk, and founded an art school and museum. He was soon involved in disagreements with the political leaders of Russia, concerning what was considered art. They were opposed to his "flying green cows and upside-down girls" and pressured him to leave Vitebsk. Constantly meeting with disapproval of his "floating figures" in his paintings, he emigrated to Berlin in 1922, where he began work on his autobiography, *Ma Vie*.

Marc Chagall

Remaining in Berlin long enough to have his memoirs published, he relocated to Paris, where he was commissioned by the art dealer Ambroise Vollard to create illustrations for Nikolai Gogol's book *Dead Souls*. Vollard later supported Chagall's travels to Israel in 1931 to search for themes for an illustration of the Bible.

In 1952, he visited Israel again, where he began a new medium of art, stained glass. He designed twelve stained glass windows, symbolizing the twelve tribes of Israel, for the synagogue at Hebrew University near Jerusalem. Other works of his include mosaics for the First National Bank plaza in Chicago, ceiling decorations for the Paris Opera, and stained glass windows for the United Nations in New York City. Chagall made his home in France after World War II and died there on March 28, 1985.

81. GEORGIA O'KEEFFE
(1887–1986)

Raised on a small family farm near Sun Prairie, Wisconsin, Georgia O'Keeffe went on to gain international notoriety as a leader of the semi-abstract style of art. Born on November 15, 1887, she was the second of seven children. At eighteen, she began formal training at the Art Institute of Chicago, transferring to the Art Students League in New York City two years later. Although she won prizes for her work, she felt "unoriginal" and quit school, destroying all the work she had completed as a student. She worked as a freelance commercial artist for four years.

Deciding to become a teacher, leaving her spare time to paint, she became supervisor of art in public schools in Amarillo, Texas, in 1912 and taught summer school at the University of Virginia. In 1914, she took a year off to attend Columbia University in New York and studied under Arthur Dow, developing her personal style. Later, talking about the inspiration she received from Dow, she called him the man "who affected my start, who helped me to find something of my own." She returned to Texas in 1915 and taught at the West Texas Normal College until 1918.

Painting and drawing again, she sent numerous abstract pictures to a friend, Anita Pollitzer. Anita took the pictures, among them the watercolor *Blue Lines Number 10* (1916), to Alfred Stieglitz (see no. 64), a photographer and owner of the gallery 291, where the work was immediately exhibited. O'Keeffe had her first solo showing at 291 in 1917 and at the same time began posing for a series of photographs for Stieglitz. Her first major exhibition came five years later at the Anderson Gallery in New York. The show was called One Hundred Pictures, and all the paintings were unsigned and untitled. She believed that "any personal quality in a picture should be signature enough."

At age thirty-seven, she married Stieglitz. The famous pieces of this period were *Black Iris* (1926) and *Two Calla Lilies on Pink* (1928). The works, famous for their closeup view of a single subject, emphasize her use of voluptuous organic forms, finding in nature corresponding images for emotional states.

In 1929, she began to travel to New Mexico. Flowers were difficult to come by in the arid climate, so she began painting bones, starting a new series, which included *Cow's Skull—Red, White and Blue* (1931). She was almost seventy years old when she took a three-and-a-half-month trip around the world. The trip inspired a new series of paintings, depicting what she viewed from the air, such as *Sky Above Clouds* (1965), which is 24-feet (7-m) wide. Although she preferred imagery to words, O'Keeffe published her autobiography, elegantly illustrated, in 1976.

Georgia O'Keeffe

His obituary read, "He used the materials of art to poke fun at its serious ideas." American painter and photographer Man Ray born Emmanuel Radnitsky on August 27, 1890, in Philadelphia, Pennsylvania, started painting at age five, although his parents, Russian-Jewish immigrants, disapproved and urged him to pursue architecture or engineering. His autobiography, *Self Portrait* (1963), describes how he stole tubes of oil paint for art.

He won a scholarship to college in architecture due to his excellence in mechanical and freehand drawing, but he declined it to go to New York City. He held a variety of jobs, first as an apprentice to an engraver, then in an advertising office. He then did layouts for a publicity firm and later was a mapmaker for an atlas publisher. In the meantime, he enrolled in night courses at the National Academy of Design and at the Ferrer Center.

He visited art galleries in the city during his lunch hour, meeting Alfred Stieglitz (see no. 64) at his gallery 291. Stieglitz introduced him to photography and to the work of the modern European artists, including Paul Cezanne (see no. 48). At that time, Ray was influenced by romanticism in art, as evidenced in his landscape paintings *The Village* (1913) and *The Hill* (1913). In 1915, he met the artist Marcel Duchamp (see no. 79), and Ray joined the dada movement. Interested in provoking public participation in his expressions, Ray hung one of his canvases by its corner, forcing the audience to straighten the picture in order to see it. Bringing dadaism to New York, he helped found the Society of Independent Artists, where for a fee of two dollars, artists could exhibit whatever they chose. Avant-garde and revolutionary, Ray mounted a series of collages on a turnstile so they could be viewed in sequence to the end. He titled the series *Revolving Doors* (1916).

In 1918, he made his first photographs,

Man Ray

which he airbrushed on, and he labeled them aerographs. In Paris three years later, he developed Rayographs. The technique involved placing objects on light-sensitive paper to produce a ghostlike imprint, making the camera unnecessary to his work.

Arousing curiosity with his changing style, Ray took his famous photograph *Violin d'Ingres* in 1924, in which the sound holes of the violin were painted on the back of a well-known model named Kiki.

In the early 1930s, he experimented with the process known as solarization. He exposed a photographic negative to light so that the background would be bleached, while the object was left with a dark, jagged edge. These photographs resembled paintings, and Ray published them in the book *The Age of Light* (1934). Man Ray died in his sleep on November 19, 1976, in his Paris studio.

Naum Gabo

Naum Gabo changed his name from Naum Pevsner to avoid confusion between himself and his brother Antoine Pevsner, who also became a renowned sculptor and painter. A sculptor and leader in the Constructivist movement, Gabo, born on August 5, 1890, completed high school in Russia, the place of his birth, and enrolled at the University of Munich, Germany, to study medicine, natural science, and engineering. His interest in art surfaced after he attended lectures by the art historian Heinrich Wolffen and visited an exhibition by the artist Wassily Kandinsky (see no. 66). By 1914, he was resolved to study art and executed his first sculpture, *Negro Head* (1914). Soon after, he left for Norway to avoid being drafted into the army. It was in Norway

that he had his first exhibition in 1916.

His engineering training was evident in his sculptures, which displayed mathematical precision. He experimented with wood, cardboard, and metal in his work, such as in *Bust* (1916) and *Head of Woman* (1916).

Returning to Russia after the war, he hoped the government would be receptive to his avant-garde art. He was made co-editor of the official art magazine *Izo*, and exerted a great deal of influence at the state art school. Faced with a shortage of wood and metal in Russia, he incorporated celluloid and clear plastic into his structures. By 1920, Gabo's art was under political scrutiny by the state, to which he retaliated by writing the *Realistic Manifesto*. The *Manifesto* stated the central values of constructivism, saying, "Art has its absolute independent value and a function to perform."

Government opposition to his art forced him to move to Berlin in 1922. He remained there for ten years and lectured at the Bauhaus School of Art. While in Germany, he further developed the use of plastic and glass in his sculptures to convey a sense of space. Most notable was *Project for a Monument for a Physics Observatory* (1922).

After Nazi guards plundered his studio in 1932, Gabo relocated to Paris, where he joined the Abstraction Creation group. In 1946, he emigrated to the United States, where he was able to execute sculptures on a grand scale, such as the aluminum, bronze, plastic, steel, and gold wire piece entitled *Constructivism Suspended in Space* (1950). He was commissioned for several sculptures and was written about in popular national magazines. In 1971, he received an honorary knighthood from Queen Elizabeth II of England. After his death, the magazine *Art News* wrote, "He created a brilliant series of transparent constructions that gave tangible form to light, space, and movement."

A Spanish painter and sculptor whose surrealist works combined elements of reality and fantasy, Joan Miró, born on April 20, 1893, came from a family of craftsmen. His father was a goldsmith, and both his grandfathers were blacksmiths. Drawing pictures at age eight, he began formal training at age fourteen at La Gonja Academy of Art in Barcelona, Spain, the city of his birth.

Pressured by his father to abandon art for a more stable career, Miró took a job as a store clerk when he was seventeen years of age. The long hours taxed his strength and he suffered a nervous breakdown. He recovered at his parents' home and enrolled in another art school in 1912, where he was taught by Frances Galí. While at the school for three years, he discovered the works of the artists Claude Monet (see no. 50) and Vincent van Gogh (see no. 56). It was at this time that he painted his first self-portrait, in which his style depicted the influences of the impressionists and the les fauves, renowned for their use of bright colors.

In 1918, he had his first show, sponsored by the art dealer Lluís Dalmau. The success of the exhibit enabled him to visit France, where he met the artist Pablo Picasso (see no. 71). In 1923, he was introduced to surrealism, which pervaded his work from then on. The paintings *The Farmer's Wife* (1923) and *The Carriage Light* (1923) are representative of his uniqueness, in which memory and the irrational are creative forces. His dreamlike paintings contain a whimsical quality, by featuring playful and distorted animal figures, twisted organic shapes, and odd geometric constructions. The forms of his paintings are organized against a neutral background, whereas the subject is displayed in bright color.

The aim of the surrealists was to denounce tradition and perform outrageous acts to shock the upper class. The group, including Yves Tanguy and Max Morise, would parade down the street shouting defamations against society and the state. At that time, Miró painted his most celebrated piece, *Dog Barking at the Moon* (1926), which has been interpreted as a symbolic link between the physical world and the world of the intellect.

Around 1934, his work became political in its support of Spain's stand against fascism. He worked for five months on the painting *Still Life with an Old Shoe* (1937) to demonstrate his empathy for Spain's poorer citizens. Dividing his time between France and Spain, Miró began to create sculptures, the most famous of which was *Woman*, completed in 1941 and over 41 inches (104 cm) in height.

Although he was affiliated with art movements, he rejected the notion that his art was abstract. He said, "A form is never something abstract: It is always a sign of something."

Joan Miró

The son of Edward Davis, art director of the *Philadelphia Press*, and Helen Davis, a sculptor, Stuart Davis, born on December 7, 1894. He was raised among artists, including his father's close friend, the painter Robert Henri (see no. 65). Leaving high school at age sixteen, Davis enrolled in Henri's art school, where he was encouraged to draw everything and anything. An ardent jazz enthusiast, he would haunt jazz clubs and depict the musicians and his feelings in paintings. To support himself while in school, he drew cartoons for the magazines *The Masses* and *Harper's Weekly*.

At nineteen years of age, he was the youngest person to exhibit in the 1913 Armory Show in New York, where a conglomerate of modern artists from Europe and the United States showed. He described the event as "the greatest single influence I have experienced in my work" and resolved to become a modern artist from that moment on. Adopting the style of the impressionists, he had his first solo show at age twenty-three, where he exhibited *Gloucester Terrace* (1916) and *Multiple Views* (1918), both landscapes. The next year he took a job as a mapmaker for the Army Intelligence Department during World War I.

In 1921, Davis became the first artist to use a commodity, a pack of cigarettes, as the entire subject of a painting. *Lucky Strike* was described as a "collage in paint." The painting was the precursor of the pop art movement of the 1960s. The critics responded favorably, leading to his further development of abstract painting. In 1927, in Davis's words, "I nailed an electric fan, a rubber glove, and an egg-beater to a table and used them as my exclusive subject matter for a year." The first painting in this period was *Eggbeater No. 1* (1927). The sale of these paintings convinced him to travel to Paris, where he rented a studio for one year and painted cityscapes. Among them was *Place Pasdeloup* (1928).

Returning to the United States in 1929, he was faced with the challenge of determining what constituted "American art." An upsurge of realistic paintings of "American scenes" emerged, and Davis opposed cultural isolation in art. Politically active throughout the 1930s, he was the first to enroll in the Federal Arts Project sponsored by President Franklin D. Roosevelt. He was also a member of the liberal Artists' Union, becoming secretary of the organization in 1936 and writing articles for its publication *Art Front*.

Davis received many honors during his last years. The Fine Arts Commemorative postage stamp, designed by him, was issued by the United States Post Office on December 2, 1964. He died on June 24, 1964, leaving his painting *Switchsky's Syntax* unfinished.

Stuart Davis

An American painter and illustrator who is best known for his covers for the magazines the *Saturday Evening Post*, *Ladies' Home Journal*, *Look*, and others, Norman Rockwell painted everyday scenes in such detail that they resembled photographs. He was born on February 3, 1894, in New York City.

Rockwell began drawing as a child to compensate for his lack of athletic prowess. During his teens, he took art courses at the Chase School, a two-hour commute each way from his home.

At sixteen years of age, he quit high school to concentrate on art full time, feeling that art was the only thing that gave him an identity. He received a scholarship to attend the Art Students League to receive traditional training. Flipping a coin to determine which instructor to study with, he entered the academic drawing class of George Bridgeman, who established the precedent for his storytelling style of painting. Rockwell was described as solemn and dedicated to his work, and his peers in school gave him the nickname "The Deacon." Along with his friends, he signed a pact in blood vowing to "never cheapen their art, never do advertising jobs, and never make more than fifty dollars a week." The pact was an expression of the idealism he felt.

His works, illustrated with humor and warmth, depicted American scenes of all types, from children playing or visiting doctors' offices, to men talking in a barber shop, to teenagers at ice cream parlors. His idealized views of society and small town America, as he explained, "excluded the sordid and ugly. I paint life as I would like it to be." His paintings were vivid with color and facial expression. National magazines immediately responded.

Rockwell's instructor obtained his first commission, and Rockwell was then given a job as an illustrator with the magazine *Boy's Life*. He

Norman Rockwell

supplemented his income by doing freelance illustrations for books such as *Tom Sawyer* and *Huckleberry Finn*. His first cover for *The Saturday Evening Post* appeared in 1916, and others soon followed, elevating his national reputation. By 1969, he had painted 317 covers for *The Saturday Evening Post*.

During World War II, the Office of War Information printed and distributed Rockwell's posters depicting the Four Freedoms. His own books were also well received, including *My Adventures as an Illustrator* (1960) and *Norman Rockwell, Artist and Illustrator* (1970). Rockwell continued to portray America as he saw it and wished it to be until he died on November 8, 1978.

87. RENÉ MAGRITTE
(1898–1967)

René Magritte

Illusionary, dreamlike paintings that display a sense of wit and humor are characteristic of the surrealism of René François Magritte (ma-GREET). A native of Lessines, Belgium, he moved with his family to the town of Chatelet. It was there that Magritte's mother drowned herself in the Sambre River when he was fourteen years old. He then moved to Charleroi with his father and two brothers and took an interest in art, studying periodically at the Royal Academy of Fine Arts in Brussels, Belgium, between 1916 and 1918.

When he was twenty-four years old, he found a job as a designer in a wallpaper factory and devoted his leisure time to painting. After viewing the work of painter Giorgio di Chirico (1888–1978), especially his *Song of Love* (1914), which, Magritte later wrote in his autobiography, "moved me to tears," he began painting more vigorously and associated himself with the surrealist movement.

Magritte was a great force for the surrealist movement and marketed himself by writing letters to newspapers. He was given a contract with the Galerie Le Centaure, which held his first solo show in 1927. The show got bad reviews from critics, and he went to Paris for the next three years, where he completed the famous *False Mirror (1928)*. It is his best-known painting, and in simple form, it resembles the corporate logo of CBS TV. A magnified eye fills the entire canvas, reflecting a cloud-filled sky; the pupil is thought to be a metaphor for a solar eclipse. He also completed *Threatening Weather* (1928), in which a headless and armless female torso, a tuba, and a wicker chair, all ghostlike and painted in white, are suspended in the sky.

Active in both art and writing, he wrote articles and statements for surrealist publications, stating his feelings about the dimensions of his work. Magritte had an extraordinary gift for combining ordinary objects into something expressive of magic. His *The Therapeutic II* (1937) shows a man wearing a hat that is suspended on a nonexistent head, sitting on a beach; his torso is a birdcage with two white doves in it. Magritte wanted to see objects "spontaneously brought together in an order in which the familiar and strange are restored to mystery," as evidenced in his symbolic dismembered figures. Described as a heavyset man, he was often photographed wearing the costume of a cape and bowler hat, two items that he painted in several works.

In 1965, he painted his summation on his view of art with *Exhibition of Painting*, where an empty landscape covers the foreground, a bowler hat on a stand shaped like a chess piece is balanced by a penguin, and a cloud-filled sky is parted by a dark form.

American sculptor Alexander Calder is best known for his creation of mobile sculpture. He was descended from a family of artists. His grandfather, Alexander Milne Calder, and his father, Alexander Stirling Calder, were traditional sculptors. His mother, Nanette Lederer, was a portrait painter. Born on July 22, 1898, Sandy, as he was called by his family and friends, remembered making figures out of wood and wire at the age of five.

At age seventeen, he entered the Stevens Institute of Technology in Hoboken, New Jersey, graduating four years later with a degree in mechanical engineering. After graduating, he went through a succession of jobs, from automotive engineer to insurance investigator to machinery salesman. Gaining an interest in art, he enrolled at the Art Students League in New York at age twenty-five and studied there for three years with Kenneth Hayes Miller and Thomas Hart Benton. While in school, he received his first art job, freelancing for the magazine *National Police Gazette*. He became fascinated with the circus and used his press pass to visit the Ringling Bros. and Barnum and Bailey circuses to sketch the animals.

In 1926, he published a book of drawings he executed at New York's Central Park Zoo, entitled *Animal Sketching*. That summer, he sailed for Europe and took sketching classes at the Grande Chaumière in Paris. He also made his first wood-and-wire animal figures that moved, later known as Calder's Circus. While in Paris, he met the sculptor José de Creeft, who was impressed by his work and assisted him in exhibiting. He returned to the United States, and the Gould Manufacturing Company began to market the animal figures as "action toys," in 1927. Back in Europe, Calder was influenced by the abstract and colorful geometric shapes in the paintings of Piet Mondrian, whose studio he visited in 1930. These paintings inspired Calder's first stabiles

Alexander Calder

also known as mobiles. He also met Joan Miró (see no. 84), who had a great influence on his work.

In 1931, Calder created his first mobile—abstract sculptures with moving parts, operated by electric motors or hand cranks. He characterized these as "abstractions which resemble nothing in life except their manner of reacting." In 1934, his motorized sculpture *A Universe* (1934) was purchased by New York's Museum of Modern Art.

Calder also drew, painted, illustrated books, designed stage sets, and fought for human rights his entire life. Always a craftsman, he deliberately used the word "work" instead of "art" to describe his activity.

89. HENRY MOORE
(1898–1986)

Best known for his large, semi-abstract sculptures of the human figure in a reclining position, Henry Moore, born on July 30, 1898, is regarded by many as the most prominent British sculptor of the twentieth century.

As a boy growing up in the industrial town of Castleford, Yorkshire, he would always find material from the manufacturing plants to amuse himself with. He would find wood to whittle with his pocket knife or clay from the local pits to mold into shapes. When he was twelve years old, he won a scholarship to the local grammar school, where he heard a story in class about the great sculptor Michelangelo (see no. 11). From that time on, if anyone asked him what he wanted to be in life, Moore would respond, "a sculptor."

At the age of sixteen, Moore entered a teacher training college. He returned to his grammar school two years later as a full teacher. Called to war in 1917, he joined the army. He returned home in 1918 and applied for a grant to study at the Leeds School of Art at age twenty-one. He was content that he had waited before entering art school, stating, "I was very lucky not to have gone to art school until I knew better than to believe what the teachers said."

Moore's work came to maturity with his five reclining figures, the most famous of which is *Reclining Woman* (1930). Carved in green stone, the figure has a masklike face, while the work shows Moore's concern for bringing out the particular character of the material he uses. The work is evidence of the influence of pre-Columbian and African sculptures. He continued to produce reclining figures, fusing nature and life and suggesting a continuity that transforms the figure into a landscape of mountains, valleys, caves, and more. Later visits to Paris brought Moore into contact with the works of Pablo Picasso (see no. 71) and Jean Arp.

Moore's first solo show was attacked by the press as "immoral" due to his de-emphasis of the head and the features of the face. During World War II, he was commissioned by the War Arts Committee to make drawings of Londoners confined to shelters due to the nightly air raids. His series entitled *Shelter Sketches* (1941) depicted the spectacle of hundreds of people running for cover during the air raids. In 1946, he visited New York on the occasion of his retrospective exhibit. That same year, his daughter Mary was born. The birth of his daughter changed his motif, and he began to carve rocking chairs and compile a series of drawings on his daughter's everyday activities.

Claiming that sculpture is a never-ending discovery, he stated, "The whole of my development as a sculptor is an attempt to understand and realize what form and shape are about."

Henry Moore

An American painter known for her realistic works, Isabel Bishop portrayed straightforward views of people and city life. Many of her subjects were found around Union Square in New York City and the subway she rode to and from her studio for forty years. The experience of the subway was integral to her art. A perfectionist, her paintings sometimes took months or years to complete.

Born on March 3, 1902, in Cincinnati, Ohio, she was raised in Detroit, Michigan. Her family was poor, yet they were high-minded in their views on education, and Isabel was not allowed to interact with the neighborhood children. Lonely as a child, she began to draw, and her family allowed her to take art lessons. At twelve years of age, she began to draw from female models. She came to New York at age sixteen to continue her studies to become a commercial designer and illustrator. She spent two years at the School of Applied Design for Women, and then, with the financial assistance of relatives, she enrolled at the Art Students League to study under Kenneth Hayes Miller and Guy Pène Du Bois, former students of the artist Robert Henri (see no. 65).

During the Great Depression, Union Square in New York was a scene of rallies and soapbox orators. She would look out her studio window at the scenes and paint what she saw without adding sentimental overtones. Her figures express a feeling of mobility, which she said means "a potential for change, characteristic of American life." She painted the "leisure class," as she called them, who were the salesgirls and waitresses hurrying to work, bench sitters, drugstore customers, and pedestrians. Her marriage to the neurologist Dr. Harold George Wolff in 1934 gave her the financial security to maintain an artistic career. Their son, Remsen, was born six years later, and he went on to become a photographer. At age forty-four, Bishop was elected vice president of

Isabel Bishop

the National Institute of Arts and Letters, and she was the first woman to be named an officer since its founding in 1898. Although she was awarded the American Artists Group Prize in 1947 for her etching *Outdoor Lunch Room* (1947), the *New York Times* found her "worn subway straphangers and shopgirls to be frighteningly isolated from any sort of human situation." Similar pieces include *Two Girls* (1947) and *Waiting* (1935). In the 1960s, she continued to take her models from the street, as antiwar demonstrators filled the city.

When she was seventy-two years old she was awarded the honor of a retrospective of her work, presented at the Whitney Museum. In 1978, the lease on her studio, where she had worked for forty-four years, expired. She moved to a new studio, but said that her art would not be the same without her familiar view.

Salvador Dali

A Spanish artist from Figueras in the province of Catalonia, Salvador Dali (DAHL-ee), born on May 11, 1904, was a painter, designer, producer of surrealist films, illustrator of books, jewelry craftsman, and creator of theatrical sets and costumes.

At an early age, Dali's artistic skills were apparent, and he was encouraged by his father, a notary, who provided him with reproductions of classical art to copy.

Before he was ten years old, Dali had completed two paintings, *Joseph Greeting his Brothers* and *Portrait of Helen of Troy*. He was taught traditional art by Juan Nuñez at a municipal school of art, where he experimented with various art forms, from impressionism to pointillism. Salvador was impressionable as a child, and in his autobiography, *The Secret Life of Salvador Dali* (1942), he admitted that his behavior was always marked by episodes of violent hysteria.

At age seventeen, Dali entered the National School of Art in Madrid, where he won several prizes. During his school years, he discovered the writings of the psychologist Sigmund Freud (1856–1939), whose theory of the unconscious influenced his later style. He was also influenced by the surrealist artists and writers, especially the poet André Breton (1896–1966). He incurred the antagonism of the school authorities, and in 1924, he was charged with creating a student riot and suspended for a year. In May of the same year, he was imprisoned briefly in Figueras for alleged political activities against the government of Spain. Reinstated in school a year later, he was permanently expelled for "extravagant personal behavior" soon after. According to Dali, the expulsion was a result of his refusal to take an art history exam given by professors he felt were intellectual inferiors.

Still active in art, he had numerous exhibitions throughout Spain, and in 1925, he had his first solo show. At the time, he portrayed a variety of styles, not quite committed to one form of painting. He used realism in his *Basket of Bread* (1926) and cubism in several *Harlequin* (1926) paintings. It wasn't until 1927, when he painted *Blood Is Sweeter than Honey*, that he demonstrated his renowned hallucinatory art, focusing on "psychological obsessions." He used this term to describe his childhood memories that he held to be special.

Painting objects in desolate landscapes, which Dali described as "hand painted dream images," he called the method "critical paranoia." It is a state of mind in which reason was deliberately suspended to allow the subconscious to emerge. This is evident in *The Lugubrious* (1929), in which he presents dream imagery, and in his famous *The Persistence of Memory* (1931), where limp watches hang from distorted trees.

Always productive, he produced the films *An Andalusion Dog* (1928) and *The Golden Age* (1930). He continued working until his death on January 23, 1989.

The term "action painting," in reference to very visible brush strokes, was first applied to Willem de Kooning, an American abstract painter and sculptor. Born in Rotterdam, Netherlands, on April 24, 1904, he dropped out of school and went to work as an apprentice to a commercial art and decorating firm. The proprietors of the business recognized his talent and encouraged de Kooning to attend evening art classes, where he learned the classical skills of drawing anatomy from casts and live models. He also learned wood graining and marble techniques. At sixteen, he went to work as a decorator for a department store, but continued to attend art classes.

De Kooning had fantasized about going to the United States to become a true artist, and he stowed away in 1926 on the ship *Shelley*, which docked in Virginia. Penniless and unable to speak English, he got a job painting houses for nine dollars a day, moving to New York City a year later. For the next eight years, he earned a living doing commercial art, department store displays, sign lettering, carpentry, and painting nightclub murals. In 1935, he was persuaded to join the Federal Arts Project, a Works Project Administration (WPA) project that paid local artists to create murals for public buildings. He was commissioned to design a mural for the Hall of Pharmacy at the 1939 New York World's Fair.

Described as a man who would "choose to be uncomfortable, rather than conform to anyone else's ideas," de Kooning developed his abstract theme of art with his first paintings, *Pink Landscape* (1938) and *The Wave* (1940). In 1938, he met Elaine Fried, an artist and art critic, whom he married five years later. After meeting Elaine, he turned his attention from depicting the male figure to painting the female figure. The interest evolved into his famous *Women* series of paintings, which included *Queen of Hearts* (1943) and *Pink Lady* (1944). In 1948, he had his most controversial showing, featuring black-and-white enamel abstractions, one of which was an entirely black painting entitled *Painting* (1948). Also an instructor, he taught art at Black Mountain College in North Carolina in 1948 and at Yale University in Connecticut from 1950 to 1951.

He revolutionized American art with the new *Women* series, beginning with *Woman I* (1952). Achieving a synthesis of figure painting and abstraction, he used slashing brush strokes to create a fragmented and distorted image. The series, according to de Kooning, was "the interpretation of the figure in its ambiguous environment." Recognized for his use of soft colors, especially pink and orange, in contrast to his visible brush strokes and distorted forms, he succeeded in evoking a sense of tension in his work.

By the late 1950s, his paintings became more symbolic, where the figure was absorbed into the landscape. He also began to devote much of his time to sculpting in clay.

Willem de Kooning

David Smith

An American sculptor and painter, David Roland Smith was born on March 9, 1906, in Decatur, Illinois. After his first year of college, he dropped out to move to New York, working at various jobs, from taxi driver to carpenter. He completed two years of study at the Art Students League in New York, which introduced him to cubism and abstract art, and he intended to become a painter. The influence of that art moved him to attach bits of wood, metal strips, and objects he found on the street to his paintings. Finally, the canvas he painted on became the support for his structures. In 1930, he abandoned painting for sculpture after viewing pictures of the welded metal sculptures of the artist Pablo Picasso (see no. 71).

Smith learned to work with metal in 1925, while he was employed as a riveter in a Studebaker automobile plant in South Bend, Indiana. He produced his first sculpture at age twenty-seven from agricultural-machinery parts. He was the first artist in the United States to make welded metal sculptures. In 1934, he established a studio in a machine shop in Brooklyn, New York, called the Terminal Iron Works. He then travelled to Europe and the Soviet Union, and upon his return to the United States, he involved himself with the Works Progress Administration (WPA) Federal Arts Project. In 1937, Smith began a series of antiwar medallions, the first entitled *Medals for Dishonor* (1937). During World War II, he worked in a locomotive factory, acquiring a lifelong interest in machinery and large-scale construction. After the war, he began to create sculptures using wires and rods.

Many of Smith's sculptures, such as *Royal Bird* (1948), were metaphors for human violence and greed, showing skeletal forms of metal rods twisted around a central shape, representing an organic figure. Most impressive of his works were his *Cubi* series, begun in 1963, showing a change of style, as he set out to create "real objects" that exist in "real space," instead of illusionary objects restricted to the base of the sculpture itself. The *Cubi* works consist of large, blocklike, polished metal shapes arranged at oblique angles. Unfortunately, his life was cut short on May 23, 1965, by an automobile accident.

Magdalena Carmen Frida Kahlo was born in Mexico City on July 6, 1907, the third of six children of Guillermo Kahlo, a jewelry maker. She was introduced to art by her father, who had an interest in Mexican archeology and art. Also an amateur painter, he would take Frida with him to the park to paint. Later he taught her how to use a camera and how to develop and retouch photos.

At age fifteen, she entered the National Preparatory School, which elite youth attended to prepare for professional careers. While there, she first made the acquaintance of the painter Diego Rivera (see no. 78), who had been commissioned to paint a mural for the school. Three years later, on September 17, 1925, the day after Mexico celebrated its anniversary of independence from Spain, Kahlo was struck by a bus and paralyzed. Forced to wear a number of plaster casts to keep her still, she was unable to perform any physical activities and began to paint to free her mind from the pain.

After three years of painting self-portraits, she took her work to Rivera, who encouraged her to continue. Her paintings had broad color areas and included fantastical elements, expressing her own feelings about the accident and her inability to have children. Kahlo recuperated but was always in pain. She became politically active, joining the Young Communist Party and involving herself in workers' rallies, making speeches and attending meetings to improve the plight of Mexico's working class. In 1929, she painted her famous work *The Bus,* depicting the life of the people of Mexico. The painting showed figures differing in social class challenging stereotypes and making the statement that all people are essentially equal and deserve equal economic standing.

At twenty-two, she married Rivera, and together they traveled around the world. She never pushed for exhibitions of her work and was content to be able to merely express her feelings, although she had three showings during her lifetime. The French surrealist poet André Breton (1896–1966) arranged her New York exhibition in 1938, and Marcel Duchamp (see no. 79) arranged her show in Paris in 1939. She had her first exhibition in Mexico in 1953. Her paintings affirmed her Mexican identity, incorporating subject matter from folk art in her depictions of her personal grief with graphic imagery. The painting *Broken Column* (1944) depicts her wearing a metal brace, while her body is open to reveal a broken column in place of her spine. Her sorrow over her inability to have children is revealed in *Henry Ford Hospital* (1932), where she depicts herself in a hospital bed surrounded by a baby, a pelvic bone, and a machine. The majority of her works are at the Frida Kahlo Museum in Coyoacan, Mexico.

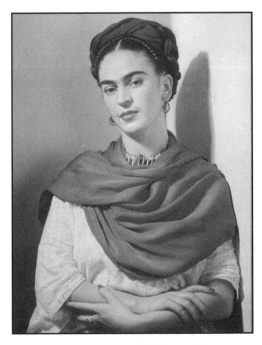

Frida Kahlo

95. HENRI CARTIER-BRESSON

(1908–)

A French photographer known for his photojournalistic reporting and a key figure in the development of photography as a documentary record, Henri Cartier-Bresson (car-tee-YAY-bress-SONE) was born on August 22, 1908. Excelling in composition, he had a unique ability to capture the fleeting moment, which he termed the "decisive moment," where the significance of the subject is revealed in form, content, and expression.

Originally interested in pursuing painting, Bresson studied art in Paris from age nineteen to twenty with the cubist painter Andre Lhote. Lhote introduced him to surrealist painting, which was to influence his photography. He didn't begin photography until 1930, when he was influenced by the works of twentieth century photographers Man Ray (see no. 82) and Eugene Atget. In 1931, he visited Africa and began taking photographs with a miniature camera. Two years later, he purchased his first 35mm Leica camera.

Cartier-Bresson's photographs have a narrative quality that combines the drama of the scene with sharp observations. He chose to record the reactions of people, rather than events, introducing a new perspective to photography. His first photojournalistic assignment was in Spain during the civil war in the late 1930s. He also found a new interest in filmmaking and assisted director Jean Renoir on three films, including *The People of France* (1936).

During World War II, he served in the French army, was captured, and spent thirty-five months in German prison camps. After three separate attempts, he escaped and made his way to Paris, where he joined a photographic unit of the Resistance that recorded the German occupation and retreat following the Allied invasion.

After the war, he moved to the United States, and in 1947, he founded Magnum Photos with the photographer Robert Capa (see no. 98) and others. It became the first cooperative photo agency. The agency compiled the work of several photographers, working worldwide, to provide photos to magazines. He served as president of the organization from 1956 to 1966.

Working in India, Pakistan, and China from 1948 to 1954, he witnessed the first six months of the change in government in the People's Republic of China. In 1954, he became the first photographer from the West to be allowed to photograph in the Soviet Union since World War II, publishing his photographs in the book *The People of Moscow*, in 1955. That same year, he was invited to become the first photographer to exhibit at the Louvre museum in Paris. His collections of photographs include *Cartier-Bresson's France* (1971), *Portraits 1932–1983* (1983), and *Henri Cartier-Bresson in India* (1988). Continuing his early love of art, he published a book of drawings, *Traits pour Traits* (Line by Line), in 1989.

Henri Cartier-Bresson

96. FRANCIS BACON
(1909–1992)

Francis Bacon, born on October 28, 1909, left Dublin, Ireland, the place of his birth, at sixteen years of age. He was a self-taught painter and set out to make a name for himself. Bacon went to London and worked at an office before relocating to Paris to work as an interior designer. While in Paris in 1927, he visited an exhibit by the painter Pablo Picasso (see no. 71), became fascinated with the paintings, and exclaimed, "Why shouldn't I try to paint?"

Returning to London a year later, he supported himself as a furniture designer and interior decorator while continuing to paint. He had an exhibit in his studio in 1930, and the magazine *Studio* published a two-page article on his showing entitled "The 1930 Look in British Decoration." His individual style is based on images of terror and anger, using bizarre subject matter to shock the audience about the violence of the human condition. He emerged on the art scene in 1933 with three abstract paintings entitled *Crucifixions*. After a series of rejections from museums and galleries, followed by the failure of his first solo show, Bacon began to gamble and lost interest in painting.

During the years of World War II, he worked as an air-raid warden in a civil defense unit. He destroyed about seven hundred paintings, dating from 1929 to 1944, because he was dissatisfied with them. He remained unknown until 1946, when he painted the "first picture I ever really liked," entitled *Painting* (1946). He intended it to be a bird hovering above a field, but the finished painting was centered around a foreboding umbrella. Now equated with surrealism, he had his first major solo show when he was forty years old. It was at this showing that he unveiled his series of paintings known as the *Screaming Popes* (1949), variations on the *Portrait of Innocent X* by the painter Diego Velazquez (see no. 25). The more than ten popes Bacon paint-

Francis Bacon

ed demonstrated his use of gruesome colors and horrifying contortions of figures. He depicted the pope with a twisted mouth, open in a scream, and adorned in a lurid purple drape, as opposed to the red normally worn by the pope. He also painted the human body based on the motion studies of photographer Eadweard Muybridge.

Exhibiting his work throughout Europe and the United States in the late 1960s and early 1970s, he began to paint his companion George Dyer in a series of daily activities. Dyer committed suicide in 1971, the year Bacon had his grand retrospective in Paris. The suicide provided the theme for Bacon's most sensational paintings, titled *Triptych, May-June 1973* (1975), which was written about in *Time* and *Newsweek* magazines. The painting depicted the figure of Dyer in a state of nausea. Painting the morbid and violent in life, Bacon said he still remained exhilarated: "When a painting, however despairing, comes out right. When I meet someone I get on well with. When I have a marvelous win."

Jackson Pollock

A pioneer of American abstract expressionist art known as action painting, in which paint is dripped on a canvas with no fixed center, Paul Jackson Pollock was a key figure in making New York City the world capital of modern art. The youngest of five boys, three of whom also became artists, Pollock was born on January 28, 1912, on a sheep ranch near Cody, Wyoming. His family was constantly moving, and he had lived in six states by the age of ten. He worked as a farmhand, milking cows, plowing fields, and harvesting crops as a boy. His free time was spent exploring the Indian ruins of Arizona, where the family settled for some time. It was in Arizona that he developed an interest in Indian sand painting.

When he was fourteen years old, the family moved to Riverside, California, where he worked as a surveyor and began to draw as a way to release tension. Entering Manual Arts High School at age sixteen, he was expelled a year later for preparing and distributing a paper entitled *Journal of Liberty*, in which he attacked the faculty for its emphasis on athletics. In 1930, he moved to New York and entered the Art Students League, studying under Thomas Hart Benton (1889–1975). The realistic painting emphasized in class bored Pollock and led to his experiments in abstract painting. At this time, he also made several trips across the country by freight train, sketching the spacious landscapes.

During the Great Depression, he incorporated his style of surrealism, where the unconscious is the focus, with cubism in his painting titled *Masked Image* (1928). This painting shows blurred and writhing images, rather than the sharp outlines characteristic of cubism. He was also employed by the Works Progress Administration (WPA) Federal Arts Project in 1935.

In 1937, he began psychiatric treatment for alcoholism. His doctor, Joseph Henderson, had him complete drawings as part of his therapy. Henderson later published these drawings in 1970 under the title *Jackson Pollock: Psychoanalytic Drawings*.

Pollock had his first one-man show in 1943, in New York, and had a show of new works nearly every year after that. Moving to the country in 1947, he began to execute his most creative works, inspiring action painting. He laid a canvas on the floor and dripped, splattered, and dribbled paint onto it. He titled these expressions *Cathedral, Number 1* (1947), *White Cockatoo* (1948), and his most celebrated, *Autumn Rhythm* (1950), where the primary color is black, the secondary is orange, with touches of other hues; the entire work lacks a focal point, as the action spreads across the canvas.

Although he was gaining acclaim internationally, he was uneasy about his fame. On August 12, 1956, while driving a car he had traded two paintings for, he struck a bump, overturned the car, and died instantly.

Photojournalist Robert Capa was born Endre Erno Friedman on October 13, 1913, in Budapest, Austria-Hungary (modern day Hungary). He was expelled from the country at age seventeen due to his active political participation in liberal groups. Emigrating to Germany, he never remained in one place long enough to call it home.

His first job, where he learned the technique of photography, was as an errand boy for the German newspaper *Dephot*. It was there that he came into contact with successful photojournalists of Germany. Holding a variety of jobs in the photographic field, he learned by watching others and borrowing cameras. His first published photograph was of Russian revolutionary leader Leon Trotsky, taken in 1931 at a meeting in Copenhagen, Denmark.

Moving to Paris for a short term, he passed himself off as a wealthy American photographer named Robert Capa. Later, emigrating to the United States as Robert Capa, he would take photographs for magazines and newspapers, obtaining three times the pay rate that an unknown photographer would.

Known for his action photographs, he saw his career lifted when he accepted a position in 1936 covering the Spanish Civil War. The photographs later appeared in *Life* magazine and brought him immediate international recognition. His most famous photograph taken during the Spanish Civil War shows a Loyalist soldier at the exact second when a bullet ends his life. His photographs were admired for their grim views of death and destruction. Capa would immerse himself in battle to capture the best images, stating, "If your pictures aren't good enough, you're not close enough." *Life* magazine commissioned him to record the events of World War II in Europe. He covered the fighting in Africa, Sicily, and Italy and also photographed the Normandy invasion on June 6, 1944. In 1948, he was sent to Palestine to record the establishment of Israel and the first Arab-Israeli war. He took the first pictures detailing the settlement of the new nation and captured soldiers in action and the actual experience of war as the fighting occurred.

Capa was also a founder of Magnum Photos with Henri Cartier-Bresson (see no. 95), the first cooperative agency for worldwide freelance photographers. In 1954, *Life* magazine offered him an assignment covering the war in French Indochina (later known as Vietnam). He took the job and was killed by a land mine on May 25, 1954, while trying to capture a scene of soldiers fighting. It is believed that he was the first American killed in that conflict.

Robert Capa

The son of a rabbi who emigrated to the United States from Poland, Leonard Baskin was born on August 15, 1922, in New Brunswick, New Jersey. American sculptor, printmaker, and book illustrator, Baskin received a strict religious upbringing. At age sixteen, he enrolled in night school at the Educational Alliance, where for five years, he studied with the sculptor Maurice Glickman and later took courses at the New York School of Architecture. He received a scholarship to study at the Yale University School of Fine Arts but was expelled in 1943 for "incorrigible insubordination." He enlisted in the navy, qualifying as a pilot, and later was a gunner in the merchant marines. While on ship, he was allowed to set up a small studio for himself, where he wrote and sculpted. On board, he completed a wood sculpture, 13-inches

Leonard Baskin

(33-cm) high, entitled *Torso* (circa 1943).

After World War II, he returned to New York and attended the New School for Social Research, continuing to voice his political opinions through his work. While in school, he executed a red oak statue of *Prometheus* (1947), representing the hardships of the working class. His social message in his work earned him a fellowship in 1947, and he also became editor of the journal *New Foundation*, which presented articles on the economic state of people in society.

During his last year of school, 1949, he abandoned sculpture in favor of printmaking for a year. He found that prints were effective in relaying social messages, and he showed his six prints entitled *Prophet* (circa 1949) at an exhibition at the Philadelphia Art Alliance. Baskin left for Europe in 1950 and had his first solo exhibition in Florence, Italy, in 1951. He showed only woodcut prints, including *Son Carrying Father* (1950). Returning to the United States a year later, he became an instructor in printmaking at the Worcester, Massachusetts Art Museum. He also established his own company, the Gehenna Press, in his home at Northampton, Massachusetts. The press produced over one hundred books, many illustrated by his prints, and remained active for twenty-five years.

Although he did not exhibit between 1952 and 1956, he continued to sculpt, incorporating the themes of death and reverence to past poets and artists in his work. The bronze *Head of Blake* (1955) was his most remarkable piece from this time and was also almost lifelike.

Communicating moral ideas through the portrayal of human figures, Baskin included loose faces, obese bodies, and spindly legs to illustrate his opinion of the spoiled condition of humankind. Other examples of his work includes *Armored Man* (1962) and *Figure* (1971).

Andy Warhol was an American painter and filmmaker who was a leader of the pop art movement because of his devotion to eliminating individuality in art. Pop art is meant to create art that is akin to everyday common life. Never discussing his life, Warhol would often make up a different background for himself at every interview. Although it is commonly thought that he was born as Andrew Warhola in Philadelphia, Pennsylvania, other records say Pittsburgh and give the birth year as either 1927, 1928, 1929, 1931, or 1932.

At seventeen years of age, he entered the Carnegie Institute of Technology in Pittsburgh to study art. To pay for his education, he sold fruit from a truck and later worked as a window decorator at a department store. After graduation, he moved to New York where he worked as an advertising artist for over ten years. He was considered to be one of the most gifted and successful commercial artist at the time. In 1957, he received the Art Directors Club Medal for a giant shoe advertisement, and it inspired him to begin to paint three years later. The department store Lord & Taylor bought his enlarged painting of the comic-strip hero *Dick Tracy* to display in their window in 1961. This launched his career as a pop artist.

According to Warhol, he painted what he did because he had no ideas of his own. He began to do stencil pictures of money because an art dealer had told him to paint whatever was most important to him. Recalling his fondness for soup, eating the same soup lunch in his mother's kitchen for twenty years, he painted rows of cans of Campbell Soup, producing *100 Soup Cans* (1962). The paintings were exhibited the next year and were noted as being his most successful commercial items. A similar famous work consisted of multiple images of film star Marilyn Monroe. Warhol defended his art by stating, "I paint things I

Andy Warhol

always thought beautiful—things you use every day and never think about."

In 1964, he established his first studio, called the Factory, where he could mass-produce assignments using a photographic silk screen process. Influenced by everything around him, he was inspired by signs and advertisements he saw in supermarkets and on the street, turning the common and mundane into art. Warhol observed that "in the future, everybody will be famous for fifteen minutes." Exploring new avenues, he began a magazine, *Interview*, which published illustrated articles about current celebrities.

Turning to filmmaking, he produced a series of movies, including *Empire* (1964?) and *The Chelsea Girls* (1966), in which there was no action or plot. He then published some of his works in the book *Andy Warhol's Exposure* (1980). In 1994, the Andy Warhol Museum, the largest single artist museum in the United States, opened in Pittsburgh.

TRIVIA QUIZ

1. Many artists have achieved fame for their self-portrait. Which artist was supposedly condemned for blasphemy by introducing his portrait onto sculpture, and which artist did actually paint his image among the famous personages depicted in frescoes for the Vatican Palace? (See pages 8 and 20)

2. What two women revolutionized the art world by joining the impressionist movement? What was the main subject of their work? (See pages 58 and 61)

3. Nicknames that allude to their profession, the profession of their fathers, the name of the people they were apprenticed to, or the place of their birth were often bestowed on artists. Which artist invented a name in order to obtain better pay? (See page 105)

4. Who was responsible for creating the symbol of authority and a model for domes throughout the Western world? (See page 18)

5. What was Andy Warhol's famous prediction for people in the future? (See page 107)

6. Photographers often capture a moment on film. Techniques are employed to capture models at their best. What techniques did Mathew Brady employ and what were the effects? (See page 48)

7. Artists often go to extreme lengths to depict a subject. What artist, famous for being the first female to receive the Legion of Honor, went to unique measures to paint her subject? What were those measures? (See page 47)

8. Individual style is important to artists. What two unique methods did Leonardo da Vinci incorporate into his famous *Mona Lisa,* and how did they work? (See page 16)

9. Few artists achieve fame in their lifetime. What was Elisabetta Sirani's fame as an artist, and how did she prove herself? (See page 34)

10. What was Hogarth's Act, and when was it established? (See page 36)

11. What label was given to Washington Allston, and what art movement did he introduce? (See page 43)

12. What artist was the only one to exhibit in all eight impressionist shows? What was this artist's motto? (See page 51)

13. What painting gave birth to the movement known as impressionism? Who was the artist? (See page 57)

14. What is pointillism? Who originated it? (See page 64)

TRIVIA QUIZ

15. Where is Mount Rushmore? Whose heads are carved on it, and what was the name of the artist that created it? (See page 74)

16. What turned Henri Matisse towards an artistic career? What term was applied to him and later to the entire group? What does the term mean? (See page 75)

17. Who created the art form known as collage? How was it created? (See page 78)

18. What Broadway musical was inspired by Marc Chagall? (See page 87)

19. What painting was the precursor of the pop art movement of the 1960s? Describe the painting. (See page 92)

20. What is action painting? To whose art work was the term first applied to? (See page 99)

21. Who was the first photographer to exhibit at the Louvre museum in Paris? What agency did he found and what purpose did it serve? (See page 102)

SUGGESTED PROJECTS

1. In our modern times it is difficult to imagine the materials artists used in the past to create art, from cavemen who used berries to make paint to the ancient artists whose only tools were primitive oil colors. To understand and appreciate the tools available to artists to express themselves, try painting, drawing, or creating a sculpture using materials normally not thought of as means to draw or paint. Some examples are ground beets as paint and burnt tree bark for charcoal drawings.

2. Many people are in awe of Michelangelo, who painted the ceiling of the Sistine Chapel on his back. To capture the feeling of this incredible feat, try to paint or draw a picture on a piece of paper taped to the underside of a table. Lie on your back and begin.

INDEX

110